Crisis Management for CORPORATE SELF-DEFENSE

How to Protect Your Organization in a Crisis . . .

How to Stop a Crisis Before It Starts

Steve Albrecht

amacom
American Management Association
New York • Boston • Chicago • Kansas City • San Francisco • Washington, D.C.
Brussels • Mexico City • Tokyo • Toronto

This book is available at a special discount when ordered in bulk quantities. For information, contact Special Sales Department, AMACOM, a division of American Management Association, 135 West 50th Street, New York, NY 10020.

Library of Congress Cataloging-in-Publication Data

Albrecht, Steven.
Crisis management for corporate self-defense : how to protect your organization in a crisis . . . how to stop a crisis before it starts / Steve Albrecht.
p. cm.
Includes bibliographical references and index.
ISBN 0-8144-0265-8
1. Crisis management. 2. Conflict management. I. Title.
HD49.A39 1996
658.4—dc20 *96-19*
CIP

Printing number

10 9 8 7 6 5 4 3 2 1

Jones and Smith had been business partners for years. Now Jones was on his deathbed at the hospital.

"I have a confession to make," he said to Smith. "I embezzled over $200,000 from our company."

"I know," said Smith.

"I sold our secret formula to our competitors."

"I know," said Smith.

"I had an affair with your wife."

"I know," said Smith.

"You know?" said Jones.

"Of course I know," said Smith. "Who do you think poisoned you?"

—Larry Wilde's *Treasury of Humor*

This book is dedicated to every business executive, owner, manager, supervisor, or employee who has said, while embroiled in a tough corporate self-defense issue, "I'm going to listen to my head and my heart and then do what's *right*."

Contents

Preface

Thanks for having the courage to read this book. And by "courage," I do mean the definition of the word at its most literal. This book was written for those readers who have the guts to say, "Planning for the serious problems that face our particular business is not about what *might* happen, but about *when* it will happen and *what* we will do about it before, during, and after."

This book should serve you best if it gets you to change the way you look at the world and thereby change the way you look at your organization. It offers a challenge to you: There are more internally- or externally-created problems facing business today than ever before.

Some of these problems never reach the light of the outside world and can be handled swiftly and successfully in-house and with little fanfare. Others, however, by their very nature and scope, burst past the doors of the company lobby and head for the nearest newspaper reporters and attorneys in sight.

Unfortunately, these kinds of problems go through a rapid metamorphosis that changes them from minor developments to full-blown crises. They also change from something that merely happens to something that must be *managed.*

There are forces—human or otherwise—lurking inside and outside your walls that want somehow to disrupt your business; the question in the 1990s is no longer *if,* but *when.*

The point to this book is not to make you hide in your office with the shades drawn and the doors locked. The real goal is to raise your awareness, empower you to act when conflict arrives at your doorstep, and know how to take small problems and wrestle them to the floor before they become big ones.

Much of what I discuss in these pages could safely be called the "unspeakable acts of business." Some of the events studied here involve product, image, employee, public relations, media, civil suit, and security problems most of us would much rather avoid, thank you. While it's always easiest to say, "I'll let someone else handle that one," or "I'll wait for that one to solve itself," some of the unspeakable acts of business must be managed, dealt with, and frankly, spoken about.

Few of us enjoy conflict and/or problems that either spring from controversy or create truckloads of discord as they grow. It is my firm belief that being an effective, courageous manager today calls for you to seek out conflict in its many forms rather than avoid it.

The flawed or even potentially dangerous product you just put on the market will not correct itself through osmosis. The resulting negative publicity connected to that product will not die out unless you help the process.

The disgruntled employee who threatens to batter his co-workers probably won't leave on his own. The employee who systematically steals from your stock room probably won't reform without intervention. The employee with a drug or alcohol abuse problem probably won't suddenly decide to get sober tomorrow without intervention.

The protesters or activists outside your building, or worse, in your lobby, probably won't go away if you ask them politely.

The plaintiff attorney representing one client or 1,000 probably won't agree to dismiss her claim against your company, even if all the evidence points in your favor.

And the publics (plural)—those people who make up your customers, consumers, business partners, vendors, observers, or critics—probably won't believe you if, when your corporate problems come to light, you first say, "We have no comment," "It wasn't our fault," or "Someone else is to blame."

All of the above events, incidents, and behaviors will definitely require intervention on your part. True corporate self-defense starts with your ability to recognize these kinds of problems and crises, understand the nature of the conflicts surrounding them, and then take as much of a proactive, rather than reactive, stance as possible. This book will attempt to arm you for any combination of the problems that may attack your company tomorrow, next year, five years from now, or, with luck, never.

> If you are engaged in commerce today, in the business of selling your products or services to customers in the marketplace, you must be aware that some risk-related episode or serious event could put your organization into a crisis mode.

With that said, let's look at the ways you can successfully defend your company *today*.

S.A.

Acknowledgments

Screenwriters often say that film is a collaborative effort. They provide the written work in the form of a script and then hordes of people take over to turn their words into images on the screen. And since every movie ends with the credits, which say to all who have viewed the work: "This is the long list of people who brought this story to you," there needs to be a similar roll of names for a book.

What follows is a short list of people who contributed their expertise, creativity and, for the most part, their listening skills to the final work you hold now. Without them, this would be much less of a book and, thanks to them, it's better than what I could have created alone.

Public relations pro Chet Burchett, senior vice president in the Chicago office of Edelman Public Relations Worldwide, takes top honors for his wide range of knowledge and his battlefield experience. He has helped many of his clients weather heavy storms and his solid crisis management expertise is woven throughout this book.

Security expert Gavin de Becker offered invaluable advice when it came to the difficult task of protecting companies from various kinds of internal and external attacks. And thanks go to former LAPD Commander Bob Martin from Gavin's office for making time for us to meet. During their careers, both men have put themselves in harm's way many times and have survived to tell the tales.

Attorney and old friend Stephen J. Fitch, from Fitch & Associates, gave me wise counsel when it came to handling lawsuits—an inevitable part of business today.

My dedicated and able researcher, Nancy Smith, gets kudos for her real-life savvy and unflagging energy. With her postgraduate degree in hand, she will make quite a mark on our world. My secretary, Irene Medlock, who kept my office from unraveling, was always thoughtful and dedicated.

My father, Karl Albrecht, himself an AMACOM author, offered his typically keen insight into this subject. His role as mentor and fellow writer makes him the greatest dad, "best practices" consultant, and two-grid model maker I know.

Passionate thanks to my wife, Leslie, who works hard as a police officer—a job filled with one creative problem-solving opportunity after another—and who still manages to juggle the demands of two active kids and an angst-ridden writer-husband.

Finally, I believe humorist P. J. O'Rourke said it best in the opening of his book *All The Trouble in the World:* "Writing this book required an enormous amount of help from friends. To them goes the credit. I'll take the money."

And certainly an ironic thanks must go to the hotel maid in Brea, California, who, not realizing the vastness of her error, threw away the box holding one year's worth of my notes, clippings, and interviews for this book. The ensuing four hours I spent waist-deep in the hotel's 12-foot trash dumpster digging through hundreds of bags of garbage for the 60-plus files that held every page of my research taught me much about the need for clear and rational thinking during a painful event.

Part One

Bad Things Can Happen, Even to Good Companies

1

The Business World as We No Longer Know It

> Every now and again, you watch a disaster unfold and seem powerless to stop it.
>
> —Treasury Dept. Chief of Staff Joshua L. Steiner, in his diary before the 1994 Senate Whitewater hearings

The message of this book is simple: times have changed, and as much as we like to avoid the notion, bad things do happen to good companies. Look out your office window and spend a few moments asking and answering the following question: "Is our world, our country, or our city any more or any less safe than it was ten years ago?"

The simple fact is that various difficult events or episodes that plague society now plague our workplaces as well. Problems that used to be exclusive to the world outside of business have now made their entry into our plants, factories, stores, and offices. And the converse is true as well: corporate problems have become part of society's problems, thanks in part to the media and the onslaught of the Information Age.

It's not always easy to accept these facts. The negative events or trying situations facing you or your firm can range from mild to life threatening. Ignoring something that's unpleasant won't make it go away. Most of us know this from experience; we've tried it, and it hasn't worked.

Ours is an increasingly unstable society. Not only do many of our more destructive problems spill over into the workplace; they can—and often do—affect the viability of the firm.

And while it's evident that we're no longer completely safe on the streets of our urban cities, it's becoming even more clear that the last bastion of safety, the workplace, is hardly free from crime, strife, or moral invasion.

It's hard to be the bearer of bad news, but our society has shown no inclination to become a kinder, gentler place, and as this book will attest—through real stories of disasters and unwanted or unforeseen difficulties—problems in the workplace have kept pace with problems in our world. To wit:

• Have we seen product tampering with deadly intent? Yes, just ask the people who make Pepsi-Cola or Tylenol.

• Do poisoned, tainted, undertested, or flawed products find their place on our retail store shelves? Yes, as has happened at Philip Morris, the Foodmaker Jack In The Box chain, Intel Pentium chips, Gerber Baby Foods, the makers of the Dalkon Shield IUD, Rely tampons, McDonald's, Similac, and Perrier.

• Have we seen corporate image disasters, either self-created or brought on by rumors? Yes, as with the still-painful public relations problems at Procter & Gamble, Intel, Snapple, Denny's, Calvin Klein, Exxon, and the Los Angeles Police Department.

• Have we seen public relations nightmares with moral and political overtones? Yes, as with AIDS activists blocking the lobbies of drug companies; abortion protesters disrupting hospitals, doctors' offices, and medical clinics; antifur demonstrators throwing blood and red paint around; and ecowarriors wreaking havoc in stockholders' meetings, forests, lumber mills, zoos, and animal theme parks.

• Do we have employees who destroy, alter, or steal data, assets, or inventory? Yes, it's a common event in many offices, retail stores, plants, and factories. What the retail industry euphemistically calls "internal shrinkage" is just another way of saying, "Someone who works for us has stolen from us."

• Do we have armed and disturbed employees killing their co-workers? Yes, as figures from OSHA, the Centers for Disease Control, the Department of Labor, and the federal Bureau of Labor Statistics will attest, over 750 people were slain in the workplace in 1992, 1,063 killed in 1993, and over 1,100 murdered during 1994. And workplace violence that does not end in homicide—threats, assaults, domestic violence, sabotage—is a hugely underreported workplace activity.

• Are there terrorist activities aimed at the workplace? Yes, as witnessed by the tremendous death and devastation following the New York World Trade Center bombing and the Oklahoma Murrah Federal Building bombing. These two events left a permanent scar on the psyche of everyone involved. The message the terrorists sent: You are no longer safe at work, no matter where you work or who you work for.

• Have we seen the sudden death of a CEO or other top company leaders? Yes, as happened to Disney when its number-two man, Frank Wells, died in a 1994 helicopter crash; to Volkswagen America when its president and vice president were killed in an airline crash; to the president of the popular Southern California hamburger chain In-N-Out, who died in a light-plane crash; and to Donald Trump, when several key members of his management team were killed in a helicopter crash.

• Can disasters like floods, earthquakes, hurricanes, and fires put an unprepared firm nearly or completely out of business? Yes, as has happened following the most recent Los Angeles-Northridge earthquakes; the Mississippi river floods; Hurricane Andrew's pass through south Florida; and any number of large and small fires that burned retail, production, or manufacturing facilities to the ground.

• Is sexual harassment still an issue in our workplaces? Yes, as witnessed by the record-setting million-dollar awards in suits brought by victim-employees of the California law firm Baker & McKenzie, Standard Oil in Texas, and Del Laboratories in Long Island, New York.

If this sounds like a litany of tales from the dark side of business, it is. Open a newspaper, pick up a national news or business magazine, or turn on the TV news, and look at what's going on in the nation around you. There are product, image, employee, crime, public relations, and lawsuit disasters cropping up at otherwise well-meaning companies every day.

The rules of the game of business have changed, are changing, and will continue to change. Today, public companies face public problems, and private companies have had their problems dragged into the public eye. Whether the crisis is brought about through fate, misfortune, negligence, or error, it can be hard to keep the press, lawyers, toxic employees, outside agitators, and just plain bad management from messing up the corporate works.

You had better be able to respond and react to any of the above-mentioned threats aimed at the sanctity of your organization and the people in it. There is no longer an impenetrable barrier between work problems and societal problems. If it happens in life, it can happen at work. This book stresses the need for ongoing, future-based event management, for problem-solving skills, for safety and security at work, and for the use of offensive and defensive public relations as today's tools for survival.

Well-known corporate security expert Gavin de Becker, who is featured in Chapter 10 of this book, puts it this way:

> Problems in the workplace are problems in society at large. Half the waking hours of most adults are spent at work. So *everything* that happens in society will happen at work. People who say of their company, "We don't have a drug problem here," are not paying attention to the world around them. If 10 percent of Americans are challenged by depression, then 10 percent of *American workers* are challenged by depression. If family abuse is a problem in society, with women and children more likely to be victimized by a family member than in the worst alley of the worst ghetto, then it's also a problem in the workplace. To believe that you have a controlled environment, a campus of some sort, where you decide who comes

in and who doesn't and where nothing bad ever happens, is a mistake.[1]

Knowing Your Company: What Is Serious for You?

The danger in a book like this starts with the fact that the phrases *business crisis* or *crisis management* can be hard to accurately define.

One dictionary refers to a *crisis* as "a decisive moment or a turning point. A crucial event, specifically the culminating point of business prosperity, following which a period of liquidation may ensue." In other words:

> A business-based crisis is an event-specific episode that can make or break you, depending upon the size of your company, the number of people you employ, the products and services you sell, and the resources of people, assets, and money you can aim at the problem.

After all, what may be a minor problem for a national chain like Wal-Mart could put your small group of shopping mall–based retail stores out of business. While your company might never have to face an issue like violence in the workplace, some large manufacturing firms have had to deal with multiple incidents within months of each other.

You may never experience product problems that would force a recall—or someone might be injured or killed as a result of using your product. And your product problems may never make the pages of your local newspaper—or they could become a leading story on national television.

You may never have to ask your insurance adjusters, attorneys, or public relations experts to help pull your firm out of a jam, or you might have to put these people on retainer or even on the payroll because the success of your business operations requires their input.

What could be a full-blown "crisis" for one company—i.e., involving the potential or actual loss of products, data, assets, goodwill, personnel, or money—might have little impact on another firm with more resources and a better plan to cope with the problem.

Since your firm is unlike any other, even within the same industry, there is no one-size-fits-all strategy for dealing with potential crises. Even the definition of a "crisis" is largely in the eye of the beholder. What *you* deem a serious problem—as opposed to a crisis—seems to depend largely upon your perception of its ability to damage or impact your firm's people, customers, and operations. This being the case, our catalog of business-crisis–related events may or may not include the kind of events or problems that could affect your business today.

But as the business community is a subset of the country and the world at large, you must be ready to react to the large problems—whether you call them "crisis" events or not—with the same kind of vigor you would the smaller ones.

It's really a question of perspective; even if you'll never have to face an episode the size of the oil-spilling Exxon *Valdez,* there are plenty of other event-specific business problems that could have just as much of a financial or personal impact on your firm.

Learning From the Best

Many companies, both those described in this book and others, have weathered difficult problems and become stronger for it. The 1982 Tylenol poisoning incident is legendary among crisis management observers, case study textbooks, and business books. While many people focus on what Johnson & Johnson did right—pulling its products, notifying stores and consumers, settling lawsuits, changing its packaging designs, working with the media, etc.—what may not be so apparent is how the Tylenol problem revolutionized product packaging in the United States.

Because a psychotic was able to alter the postproduction Tylenol, the company went to great lengths to make its new versions completely tamper-proof. And what worked well for the pharmaceutical and over-the-counter drug industry has transferred to nearly every other consumable or edible product from mouthwash to yogurt. Now, nearly every food or medicine we eat or otherwise ingest is safety-sealed for our protection.

Did other manufacturers choose to take on the added expense of changing their product packaging out of benificence or necessity? It was the marketplace, of course, that drove them to follow suit. Thanks to the Tylenol problem, customers who bought millions of consumable products began looking hard at the designs and asking, "Is this thing safe?"

Product producers reasoned (correctly, it appears) that if consumers didn't see lots of tape, fasteners, plastic guards, metal foil, caps, or other tamper-proofing devices, they might somehow assume that the product was not as safe as a competitor's.

A serious problem evolved into an opportunity to make changes for the better. One significant crisis at a very visible company led to important changes in its operating procedures. And while Johnson & Johnson and the other victims of the Tylenol event would just as soon have avoided their involvement in the whole ugly business, it did allow for a sea change in the way they serviced their customers.

As J & J's product protection evolved, consumer confidence in Tylenol soared. The message the customers heard was bell-like and stirring, "We deeply regret that this terrible thing happened. We will take bold steps to see that it never happens with our products again." One of many lessons to be learned here is that, since you can't change the past, you can and must both prepare and change for the future.

It Can't Happen Here and Other Rationalizations

The motto "We see what we want to see" is true for most organizations. As managers, we spend so much time handling various time-consuming chores, talking to our customers, and putting out the daily ration of personnel, product, and service brushfires, that we can neglect the people and events around us. It's easy to say, "I'll get to that problem tomorrow," because with luck, maybe someone else will handle it, it will go away, or perhaps it will solve itself.

And some managers are so concerned with the elements of production or order fulfillment, getting products and services to their customers, or otherwise making sure the workload gets handled, that they fail to see internal or external problems in the making.

This neglect often manifests itself not with regard to the customers, who often get plenty of attention from entire departments geared to make them happy, but with regard to the employees. Nowadays, many managers expect or infer that their people can work autonomously. Catchy phrases like *employee empowerment*, *benchmarking*, and *self-guided work teams* are on everyone's minds, so much so that some employers now take their people for granted, feeling that less guidance or hands-off supervision is better than too much. While this may suit the motivated, dedicated employees just fine, for that 5 to 10 percent of the labor force who sees the workplace as a place to get paid just for showing up—or worse, manipulating the system—the results can be disastrous.

To use a truly 1990s example, most employees with drug or alcohol abuse problems don't flaunt their behavior at work. The phrases *functioning alcoholic* or *functioning drug abuser* mean that these people can continue to use their liquor or their drug of choice and still put in an eight-hour day with you.

While drug users usually show rapid declines in their work rates, habits, and productivity, many functioning alcoholics can go on drinking and working, working and drinking, for twenty years. Since the people who work around this person will either try to rehabilitate him or her and fail, or worse, play the patsy for their drinking behavior, the alcoholic employee gets away with alcoholic work because co-workers, managers, and supervisors are too intimidated, too apathetic, or too self-absorbed to intervene and get this person professional counseling and other forms of legitimate referral help.

Sexual harassment, workplace violence, embezzlement,

theft, vandalism, and other often "hidden" company crimes start when managers and supervisors turn a blind eye to the problems. They often end only when the company gets served with a lawsuit for failing to intervene and stop inappropriate, illegal, or dangerous behavior.

Apathy, avoidance, or ignorance of personnel problems is inexcusable at the managerial or frontline supervisor levels because of the physical proximity between employees and their direct bosses. As you look higher in the firm, however, the reasons for not seeing these kinds of employee behaviors change. CEO or other top executive apathy tends to manifest itself in several ways:

- "Those kinds of things don't happen around here, at least not on *my* watch."
- "Hey, I'm not running a babysitting service here. I expect my employees to act like adults, do their work, and leave their off-the-job problems at home."
- "We pay our managers and supervisors good money to take care of that stuff. It's their responsibility to fix things. And if they don't, the fault lies with them, not us."
- "Employee problems are the responsibility of the HRD, personnel, employee assistance, or security departments. We don't deal with those kinds of things at the senior management level."
- "We tend to fly by the seats of our pants around here. If something does come up, we'll handle it then."
- "Those things happen at other companies. We've never had that kind of problem here, so we don't waste time worrying about it."

How do we account for some of these less-than-farsighted remarks? Are such executives being insensitive or unrealistic? Have they lost sight of the need to handle day-to-day problems in favor of their need to engage in long-range planning?

In some instances, the work done by the people "on the line"—that is, away from the field of view of top management—is so far removed from them that those in the executive ranks may have lost physical and ideological touch with their employees.

In organizations with many managerial levels, significant bureaucratic ranks, many policies, a noticeable lack of hands-on management, or a headquarters on one side of the country and various divisions scattered across the nation, the distance between the employee on the frontlines and the chief executive officer may literally be as wide as the nation from coast to coast.

This is not to say that the CEO needs to know the name, rank, and serial number of every employee in the company, but he had better demand that the *managers* in his employ know exactly what is going on inside and outside the company.

Of all the executive excuses, the most dangerous is the one that goes, "It could never happen here." This is the mind-set that says, "It's okay to sit back on our heels and do nothing different. It's 'business as usual' around here. We're just not one of those companies where bad things happen."

There are scores of firms who tried to use the "never happened here" rationalization as a defense for ineptitude and indecision. Their inappropriate responses to certain problems requiring corporate self-defense demonstrate that history is not always the best indicator of what's to come. In other words:

> What has happened or has not happened in the past is not an accurate indicator of the future.

Answering the Call

There's an old and cynical saying about life that certainly applies to business: "If something's bad, it happens; if something's good, it goes away." It's hard not to recognize the truth of this adage, especially if the cycle describes some crisis that has happened or is happening at your company.

And there's another of life's truisms that applies as well: "When the phone rings past 10:00 p.m., it's rarely good news."

Such is the nature of most serious corporate problems. As one veteran public relations executive puts it, "When the worst hits the fan and your company is suddenly faced with some kind of disaster, it's never on a Wednesday in the middle of the afternoon. When the phone rings with bad news, it's always a Sunday, on Easter, during a snowstorm, when your CEO and the number-two guy are on a plane for the next five hours and completely unavailable."

No matter what product or service you sell, no matter what your industry, market, or type of organization, you may face a serious corporate emergency at some point in the near future. If nothing significant has happened to you or your firm to date, consider yourself lucky. But just because you don't hear examples of modern-day disasters doesn't mean they aren't going on around you. There are many companies and their leaders who have had to fight back, and in some cases, are still fighting back, from product, image, employee, or management disasters that have threatened the health and safety of their companies' products and services, their reputation and long-term economic future, and their people.

Writing Your "Bug List": Where Are the Potential Crises in Your Company?

Psychologists and stress-management experts like to suggest that when you feel that the walls are closing in on you, you should create a "bug list." Sometimes it helps to see your problems in front of you where, at least on paper, they can begin to look a bit more manageable.

You can use this technique in the business arena by creating your own bug list. This list is not for small things like "Don't like location of coffee pot" or "Copy machine running funny." The true bug list should cover major problem areas—potential issues relating to liability with your products, services, employees, or customers, or current risk-related events that require immediate or very-near-future solutions.

When you look across the broad landscape that is your company, what is it that troubles you most? Which current or potential problems keep you awake at night? It may seem a bit bizarre to brainstorm in this manner, but there are several valuable purposes to the creation of your bug list. Your own individual list will vary according to such factors as the size and type of your firm, your role in the company (i.e., are you the owner or a manager?); the types of products and services you offer; the worklife climate and culture inside your organization; the level of implied or ongoing risk in your products or practices; and the relationship between management and the workers. Apply the following guidelines with your own company in mind:

Potential Crisis Problems, Risks, and Events

- What problems may occur with our products that will require special management skills?
- What problems may occur with our services that will require special management skills?
- What problems may occur with our employees that will require special management skills?
- What problems may occur with our customers that will require special management skills?
- What problems may occur with our outside vendors or business partners that will require special management skills?
- What kinds of preexisting plans do we already have in place to manage one or more of these events?
- Who is in charge of managing our response to one or more of these events? Is it me? Is it people above me or below me? Do we have a team of people trained to react to a variety of problems?
- What kind of training needs to accompany our management responses to one or more of these events?
- Is our company organized around a response-based chain of command, so that each person knows his or her role?

- Will we be able to manage our image properly, protect our human and company assets, and continue to serve our customers should one or more of these events occur?

These ten items should give you food for thought. Your bug list questions and problem areas could be similar to the ones above or quite different. The important point to bear in mind is that, by creating it, you've already started to consider some of the liability issues that might affect the health and viability of your company, its resources, its critical assets, and its employees.

In some organizations, the answers to some of these key questions might be, "I don't know," "None," or "No one." If these sound like your answers, it's time to put more of your energies into creating crisis response plans. You shouldn't need to search for the fire exits when the building is already in flames. Your bug list should serve as the first bell in your corporate fire alarm.

The Company as Victim: The Paralysis of Fear

Anne Wright, a senior executive of the United States Postal Service, has spearheaded her organization's search for answers with regard to its well-publicized employee violence issues. In discussing her own organization's response to violence in the workplace, she makes a thought-provoking observation that applies to any company in times of turmoil. In summary, her point is this: It's important to recognize that during and following any significant event (not necessarily relating to violence) the *victims* don't think clearly, and since the *employer* is as much a victim as the *employee,* by proxy, the *organization* doesn't think well either. In other words, the company's coping mechanism is suddenly on the fritz.

What this means is that, once they're embroiled in a significant problem, companies often make things worse for themselves, not because they mean to, but because the people at the top, who must make important decisions during and following critical incidents, can get trapped in the victim mode as well, and thus fail to respond properly.

Realizing that this is true is half the battle; knowing what to do about it is the other half.

> In times of great stress, we revert back to what we know and, more importantly, how we have been trained and conditioned to respond.

If you have some idea—and it doesn't have to be absolutely, exactly, or perfectly planned, discussed, or detailed to the nth degree—of what to do first, next, and last during any significant event, you will fare better than your counterparts or competitors, who, when faced with similar problems, will let indecisiveness, ignorance, or just plain wrong influences affect their behaviors, reactions, and responses.

In some cases, doing *anything* will at least be better than doing *nothing*. In others, doing the right combination of things will solve most of your problems. And in still others, doing everything possible correctly will still not fix the problem. But in nearly every case, it may make more sense to act decisively, even in the face of uncertainty, than to wait for the perfect solution that may not yet exist.

Having a plan for responding to a significant business problem or true crisis and then never needing it is like paying on a life insurance policy when you're in perfect health; you just never know what the future holds.

Note

1. In-person interview with Gavin de Becker, December 14, 1994, Studio City, California.

2

Business as a Target

Working in the Age of Entitled Disgruntlement

> The fire at the manufacturing plant was due to friction caused by a large inventory rubbing up against an insurance policy.
>
> —Old business saying

It's time to focus on the reasons, excuses, abuses, complaints—hidden or otherwise—that create the problems that can lead to crises in organizations. The conflicts, problems, or other impending disasters that arise from inside and outside an organization are often created by people, groups, or entities with their own agendas. Some of these people dwell inside the organization, others outside it. In either case, they may have more than charity and goodwill on their minds.

The "toxic" manager or employee who goes around the company destroying its physical or psychological assets may have an agenda that is personal, secret, and volatile.

The disgruntled customer who races to the first lawyer he can find who will take his case may be more interested in a nuisance settlement from you than in real justice.

The activists who protest at your doorsteps will have a very vocal agenda—publicity for their cause, the need to express their anger over what they feel is corporate greed or apathy, and the desire to create change through the infliction of real pain or other media-generated discomfort.

These are just a few examples of people or groups who might go out of their way to disrupt the relative harmony that is your corporate world. Forces in our society, human or otherwise, can come together to put certain companies into difficult, compromising, or embarrassing positions.

When a rumor starts in one city that McDonald's puts worms in its hamburgers, the company cannot ignore the possible fallout of this spurious news. Chapter 1 explored *what* can go wrong and how it can affect any company; this chapter focuses on *who* can cause these events and why.

Agendas: Who Has Them, Hidden or Visible

Agendas are like opinions about politics; everybody has one. And by several definitions, an *agenda* is like a set of marching orders people carry around in their heads: goals, plans, or ideals that motivate them to do certain things; or a guiding force that steers their behavior in various directions to meet their own needs.

However you look at it, the country is full of people with their own agendas, some of them positive, others not so nice; some very apparent, some not so evident.

Visible or not, the need for recognition, money, or a pound of flesh drives many people, either alone or in groups, to go after our institutions: government, politics, schools, law enforcement, the courts, the media—and, of course, business.

During any significant event that affects company operations, it's difficult to look outward at the root causes of the problem. Much of the energy and time committed by the company's leaders goes to finding the most appropriate solutions. While that's certainly an appropriate use of management's time and talents, it helps, in the aftermath, to be able to step back and ask an honest question: "Was this problem created by people, an accident, or an event related to or unrelated to our current work with our products, services, or customers?"

If the cause of your current problem is associated with some form of human intervention—a lawsuit, a strike, a security problem, a boycott, a protest, or an attempt to bring your firm into the media limelight, you should ask another important question: "If outside people or disgruntled employees are at the root of this problem, what is their agenda?"

Your last questions are even more important ones: "Will our various responses to this problem advance, hinder, or have no effect on their agendas? And what will our responses do to further our own agendas as a company?"

We can play devil's advocate and look at the people-generated events already listed with these ramifications in mind. There are other examples beyond the ones chosen, but these will do for the purposes of examination. In terms of agendas, consider these events, your company's choice of responses to them, and the end results:

A Lawsuit

Here the primary goal of the plaintiff may be money—your money. The secondary goal, however, may be exposure, publicity, media attention, or the desire to stick a thumb into your collective eye. While the suit's initiator(s) will probably not turn down a cash settlement, money may not be the only issue if their goal is to try to embarrass or humiliate your firm in a courtroom (and in that other popular, media-driven facade known as the "court of public opinion").

As we will see in Chapter 9's coverage of lawsuit protection, settling a nuisance civil suit early may *not* be the best strategy, especially when it comes to your firm's reputation. Trying your case in the newspapers may not pay many dividends either, but there is much to be gained by taking a defensive stance that says, "We will fight for our rights now, not two years from now when this case finally goes to trial."

If you can determine what the other side's agenda is at the preliminary stages of any suit, you can set up a defense based on early action rather than taking the usual "no comment, we'll wait for a court date" stance that so many companies seem to choose as their only way out.

A Strike

If your labor problems have deteriorated to such a state that a strike is inevitable, you have little choice but to continue operating the company using every legal means possible. For some CEOs, that means making the hard decision to hire replacement workers.

Agendas become complicated in labor union struggles. The hidden agenda of the union may be out of sync with the one actually voiced by its members. While the union heads may want publicity, exposure, and a chance to show how they can manipulate or control the talks with management, most union employees usually just want to go back to work. Your efforts to enhance your position in the public eye by stating, "We want everyone back on the job and we want to get our firm back to full productivity," can do more than simply saying, "There are no new talks scheduled."

A Security Problem

Security issues inside companies are usually shrouded in secrecy. Few firms want to air their dirty laundry in public. Company leaders reason that any apparent breach of security—e.g., a theft ring, violence, vandalism or sabotage, lost or stolen information, etc.—will make them look weak or out of control.

And while it may make perfect sense to keep the handling of these matters confidential, it may help to publicize your reactions to certain security problems with an eye to sending the right message to the current or future perpetrators and victims.

The company that admits that its computer files were "hacked" and then publicizes new antihacking, antivirus security measures tells other people, "We're concerned about this new crime and we want to stop it from harming us ever again."

With domestic violence in the workplace becoming a visible issue, some firms have publicized their involvement in awareness and prevention campaigns. The list of concerned organizations includes Polaroid, Liz Claiborne, Ben & Jerry's, Reebok, Marshall's, VF Corp., and DuPont.

A Boycott

The agenda of most boycott movements is clear from the start: "Give us as much news coverage as possible while we engage in this behavior." Fortunately, for most midsize to large firms, a sporadically organized boycott will have few harmful effects, especially if the media refuse to fuel it.

However, the boycotts set up by organizations with their own agendas—not strictly related to creating a decline in the sales of your products or services—can be very damaging to your reputation. This includes calls for boycotts from large and powerful minority group organizations (the Urban League, the NAACP), special-interest groups (the National Rifle Association), religious organizations (the Christian Coalition), and political action committees (AIDS groups, the National Organization for Women, etc.)

In cases where it's not just some irate customer who threatens to switch from your house paint to your competitor's, there can indeed be tremendous ramifications associated with negative publicity. Unlike lawsuits, where a good offense may be the best defense and vice versa, it sometimes pays to admit your faults, settle the dispute, and move on. Coors Brewing Company, Denny's Restaurants, and other high-profile companies have learned this lesson in recent years.

A Protest

Protesters want media coverage first and foremost. Then they want to feel the satisfaction of having disrupted your business operations and activities for an hour, a day, a week, a month, or a year. If there is little media coverage, there won't be much continued disruption. Understand the agenda of most protest groups—"Give us a reason to justify our existence"—and you'll soon discover how best to thwart them. Unlike boycotters, who call for a complete national or local halt to the use of your products or services, protesters are often more interested in enhancing their image.

Since you can't fight them on their terms (unless you want to see your executives pointing fingers at angry protesters on the evening news), the best way to handle their agenda is to ignore it. After all, you don't see the United States ambassador coming out of his or her office to address the masses every time some band of agitators pickets one of our overseas facilities. Instead of fighting fire with fire, as in civil suit protection and security issues, fight fire with apathy.

People or Groups Who Use the Media as a Mudslinging Device

As public relations expert Chet Burchett will discuss in Chapters 7 and 8, the best way to get the media on your side is to have them on your side in the first place. The agenda of the mudslinger is to make your firm look disreputable, dangerous, or even hazardous. If you help the media see that your reputation is sterling, your products and services are top quality, and your policies and procedures for handling your employees and customers are fair and equitable, you'll be way ahead of the mudslingers.

Most reporters, TV news people, and radio interviewers are bright enough to realize when they're being manipulated by some group or person with an agenda. When they know the real score, they will not help mudslingers hurt you. How you handle your company's reputation, and what type of appearances your top people make in print, on radio, and on TV can go a long way toward swaying public opinion for or against your organization.

The media is becoming *more* pervasive in our lives, not less. People with hidden or visible agendas already know this. How about you?

Employee Entitlement: The Justification for Everything

And just as we live in the Age of Disgruntlement, we live in the Age of Entitlement at work (and in all the other parts of our lives).

> Where the disgruntled employee tells all who will listen, "I hate this place and it's somebody's, anybody's fault but mine," the entitled employee says, "I *deserve* this and I *deserve* that . . . I'm entitled to those things and I want them. If I don't get them, I might quit, sue, lash out at you, or just take what I want."

On the job, the psychology of entitlement says that individuals believe it's not their fault if their expectations aren't met by either their actions or experiences. Society, the company, their co-workers, the boss—it's these institutions or people who are really to blame.

Contrast this with the idea of the great American work ethic, which today seems almost archaic to some employees. For some people, the old approach—pull yourself up by your bootstraps and you can make a better life at home and at work—is fast being replaced by the new work ethic that says, "I'm underpaid, underappreciated, and underrespected. This company doesn't demonstrate any loyalty to me so I don't feel any loyalty back. As far as I'm concerned, thanks to downsizing and this economy, I'm two weeks or less away from my next job anyway."

And so the growth of this belief leads some employees (and not necessarily the marginal or grossly unethical ones) to believe that their company owes them more than a paycheck. This belief leads in turn to such at-work behavior as coming in late and leaving early, stretching lunches and breaks, talking for hours to the opposite coast on the Internet, and misusing or misappropriating the company's psychological assets, time, or property.

During my discussion with a man who worked as a machinist for a large shipbuilding firm, I asked him if his co-workers ever stole tools or materials from the company. "Oh, yeah," he said, "it happens all the time over there." He proceeded to run down the list of items that left in lunch pails, backpacks, and under coats every day.

And when I asked him why he thought the workers stole so much from the company, he became angry and said, "Because we haven't had a raise in seven years!"

Sociologists and psychologists have coined the term *social proof* to describe the use of certain perceived social behaviors as justification for their own, similar behaviors—i.e., "It's being done by others around me, so it must be acceptable." Therein lies the key to why some people steal from their employers, drink on the job, fight with their bosses, or sue the company for the slightest indiscretion. Your awareness of excuses and abuses should be based on the premise that a few marginal people will justify their actions in this way. In terms of corporate self-defense, such people may also be the ones who cause you the most problems. The old 80-20 rule seems to apply here: 20 percent of your employees will cause 80 percent of your problems. You can complain about these head-pounding statistics, or you can do something about them. Beating the excuse monger at his or her own game calls for your organization to make positive changes in the company culture and climate, or make selective changes in the employee rolls (getting rid of the unproductive, constantly complaining, deadwood types tomorrow), or both.

It is the psyche of entitlement that permits unacceptable employees to justify their unproductive or even destructive behavior on the job. Here are just a few examples:

AN EMPLOYEE OF A NEON SIGN SHOP was fired for being late nearly every day of his 10 years on the job. He filed a lawsuit against the shop, saying that his tardiness and absenteeism was due to a subconscious fear of being on time. The shop owner lost and was forced to pay a large award to the man.

A GAS STATION OWNER fired a mechanic for working while drunk and smoking marijuana on the job. The terminated employee somehow convinced a state labor board that his drug and alcohol use was stress- and job-related. The owner ended up paying $3,000 for the mechanic's stint in a chemical dependency center.

A UNION EMPLOYEE brought a gun to his job, pointed it at a co-worker, and pulled the trigger. The gun misfired and the man was later overpowered by other employees. He was later found to have a history of mental illness and substance abuse. After completing a series of treatment programs, the man came back to work and was given limited-duty jobs because his original position had been phased out.

When he was let go because he was thought to be a safety risk, a union arbitrator ruled that he should be allowed to come back to work because the company was legally obligated under the Americans with Disabilities Act to help him treat his substance abuse, violence, and psychological problems.

The business trade publications and labor law newsletters are full of such incidents, wherein the needs of the employer conflict expensively with the rights of the employee. And when you hear stories like these, it's hard to have much hope or feel that you are in control of your own company.

As the debate rages on, both sides will have to find a common ground. After too many companies are forced to pay outrageously excessive labor law damages, someone will finally stand up and say, "Enough is enough." Since that time is not at hand, you can only arm yourself with the best information about the latest trends in employment law, and keep your hiring, discipline, and termination practices as close to the current legal guidelines as possible.

Toxic Companies: Managers and Employees in the Culture of Hate

The best companies and their leaders have focused their efforts on the ongoing development of a healthy culture. And a strong culture is a self-fulfilling animal; the more people feel protected, nurtured, and empowered—i.e., happier about what it is they do, who they do it with, who they do it for, and why they do it at all—the harder they will work. And the harder they work, the more the company rewards them for their efforts. (To continue this last point, when was the last time you heard about a company paying a performance bonus to a bunch of miserable employees?)

Of course, all this talk of the need for a healthy culture conveniently ignores the opposite side of the scale: the toxic company culture. Here, the employer is at odds with the employees. There is little sense of community, spirit, or teamwork in the organization. Loyalty and the concepts of working together for the greater good of all are out the window. Management eats in one cafeteria, the frontline eats in another. People in adjoining departments treat each other like competitors, haggling over chores, backstabbing each other with spurious information, and otherwise sabotaging internal service relationships.

In a toxic culture, jobs are designed to create as much stress in the employees as possible; policies and procedures are written and enforced to punish the employees for their errors rather than reward them for their successes; and the employees are spoken *at* and treated as if they are the root cause of what's wrong in the company. Issues like employee participation, mentoring, empowerment, and feedback are thought to be too "soft" to be addressed by top management.

From the customer's point of view, the toxic company culture has an "everyone for himself/herself" feel to it. Since communication is in jeopardy, the customer may feel as if he or she is receiving uneven or unpredictable treatment. The employees are so busy dividing into cliques, bickering with management, or fencing off their various fiefdoms, that no one much cares about the lowly customers and their not-so-important needs.

It's safe to say that this archetype of the toxic company doesn't exist in its purest form, largely because no firm could operate entirely at that level and still survive. But thanks to inept, ignorant, and insensitive management types, some firms offer up a pretty fair imitation of the perfectly toxic organization.

Peter Halmos started a company called SafeCard in 1969,

offering credit card holders a way to register their cards and be notified if they are lost or stolen. In 1992, as former AT&T Universal Card president Paul Kahn looked at an offer to lead the firm, he found a prime example of the kind of toxic workplace that can drive good employees to the exits in droves. As one business magazine article put it:

> Halmos's SafeCard had become a company obsessed with security. Every employee was searched as he or she exited SafeCard headquarters in Cheyenne, Wyoming. The building was controlled by fingerprint identification systems. Armed guards roamed the halls. It was not an atmosphere that encouraged innovation or risk-taking. Amidst hostility and dissension, Halmos finally left in 1992. Kahn quickly fired all eight top managers and got rid of Halmos's overblown security. "You can't have top-quality service if employees don't feel valued," Kahn said.[1]

With no evidence of sensitivity toward its employees' needs or concerns, no visible leadership skills exhibited by top management, and no sense that the quality of worklife in the organization is critically important to its success, these toxic organizations can roll along unchanged for years.

Worse yet, the leaders of the same companies—companies that are often struggling in their markets, losing money consistently, and failing to satisfy their shareholders—are quick to find fault with every other thing. For them, the employees—who don't work hard enough in the first place—are largely to blame for the company's rousing lack of success. Other culprits include the government, the economy, the competition, the R&D department that failed to find the flaws in the product, or the customer service department that chased away the firm's most important client.

The fault in the toxic company lies not so much with its people but with its culture. The healthy, nourishing culture develops healthy, nourishing employees. This is not to say that every day has to be like a stay at Disneyland, just that top management must send a message down through the layers of the organization that says, "We care as much about our people as we do about making money. If we don't take care of them, they won't take care of us."

As we will see in subsequent chapters covering internal crises, the toxic company's culture usually has much to do with the firm's mishandling of events. Culture is a thermometer in the organization; your ability to take the company's temperature from time to time (using attitude surveys, feedback questionnaires, and conversations with your people and their customers) can help you make the right kind of decisions.

Note

1. Koselka, Rita, and James M. Clash, "Filling the Founder's Shoes," *Forbes*, January 30, 1995, p. 99.

3

Product Disasters

If it's stuck, force it. If it breaks, it needed replacing anyway.

—Old Navy saying

With physical products that customers or other public consumers buy and use or buy and eat, the risk of a disaster is always on the horizon. Yet considering the billions of products sold in the United States every year, it's amazing that there aren't *more* problems.

Thanks to companies that use strict production, manufacturing, and packaging techniques, the incidence of problems—through tainted, sabotaged, poisoned, or flawed products—is thankfully low.

Still, these cases do exist, and the biggest ones make the news headlines with sudden alacrity. Much of this publicity is for good reason, especially if the use of that product—as with the 1982 Tylenol incidents and the 1993 Jack In The Box food poisoning cases—causes death.

As a consumer society, we tend to take product quality and safety for granted. The United States is the leading manufacturer of goods in the free world. In third world countries, where ingredient lists are suspect, testing, quality control, inspection, and evaluation are often nonexistent. As a result, problems relating to the health and safety of meats, fruits and vegetables, packaged foods, and medicines are well-known and wearily accepted by native consumers.

In the United States, when a product fails, a medicine has something seriously wrong with it, or a food we like to eat turns out to be life threatening, it's front page news and rightly so.

The benefits of this kind of exposure are many: it alerts customers that something is amiss with the product and that they should therefore pay careful attention to what they buy until the problem has been resolved. It instantly tells the manufacturer and its distributors that there is a serious problem that calls for an immediate, planned, and careful response to a potentially difficult situation. It alerts various governmental watchdog agencies, like the Food and Drug Administration (FDA), the Federal Trade Commission (FTC), the Commerce Department, and the Occupational Safety and Health Administration (OSHA) that review procedures and possible intervention steps may become necessary.

But because the Tylenol incident served as the benchmark for all product problems to follow, companies can no longer claim ignorance or wail aloud, "Now what do we do?" The seeds for their necessary product "recovery" have already been sown by companies who have had to go down this hard road before them.

Saving Similac: Fast Action and Help From the Media and Uncle Sam

One recent success story following the discovery of a flawed product comes from Abbott Labs, makers of the Similac baby formula.

This popular infant nutriment sits on store shelves in cans, in both powdered or liquid form. Similac is one of the industry leaders in the highly competitive and multisegmented baby foods market. The company sells its products to new parents, who can be understandably concerned about the type and quality of the foods they feed to their infant children.

In January 1995, the company found itself facing an odd kind of product-tampering incident, one that involved the direct sale to retailers of a *counterfeit* version of its powdered formula in California. Here was a case, not of someone tainting or poisoning the original product, but of a criminally minded entrepreneur recreating it and trying to pass it off to retailers and consumers as the legitimate item.

Suddenly the makers of Similac faced a crisis: someone was actually attempting to duplicate the label, can, consistency, taste, color, and more important, the *price* of Similac's powdered infant formula.

Several grocery store chains and a number of independents bought the fake formula from the counterfeiters and then stocked it on their shelves as the real thing. When the stores, and later Abbott/Similac, began to field complaints about the quality of the formula, the company began to investigate.

What it found was powder and cans that looked like its own, but that were clearly counterfeits. The labels were poorly printed and the color of the powder was not the same as the original.

Freeze-frame here for a moment and put yourself in the shoes of a parent who has just fed his or her son or daughter a helping of this fraudulent formula. Imagine how you would feel if you gave your baby something made by crooks out to rip off the product of a bona fide manufacturer.

To their credit, the makers of Similac didn't hesitate. They sent their representatives out to seize the counterfeit formula from store shelves and later, helped the FDA launch an investigation into this odd but potentially devastating event.

To its credit, the FDA, which has its own sworn police force of gun-carrying investigators, swooped into one California city suspected of housing the fake formula operation and made several arrests.

Before these arrests were made, the real makers of Similac offered plenty of assistance to the federal representatives, the store retailers, their distributors, and most importantly, to its customers.

In many California cities, once the TV stations and newspapers got wind of the fake product, they ran several quasi-public information stories warning consumers about the counterfeits and showing the differences between the real stuff and the phonies. In effect, the media helped Abbott Labs to spread the word so effectively that the company came out looking like an innocent victim in the whole ordeal—something that hasn't always happened in other product disasters.

So, with the media helping the company to spread the word, the FDA's arrest of the culprits, and Abbott Labs handling calls and questions from its customers, all the right bases got covered. In the end, the company lost no market share and may even have improved its image—going from a large, "faceless" manufacturer to a more human, customer- and baby-friendly firm. Consumers in general, and Similac customers in particular, got to see the company respond to this event in an entirely positive, truthful, and open way.

Once the incident was resolved about one month later, Tom McNally, president of the Ross Products Division at Abbott Laboratories, published an open letter to his customers that ran in many California newspapers. Here's the letter in its entirety:

> As the makers of Similac, America's leading infant formula, we at the Ross Products Division of Abbott Laboratories take safety and quality seriously. Our ultimate customers—the babies of California, the U.S., and the world—are too important to take any chances. That's why we perform nearly 2,000 tests to assure the quality of every batch of Similac we make. We value the trust that you've given us for so many years.
>
> Individuals recently took advantage of that trust by manufacturing and selling California retailers a powdered substance in counterfeit Similac cans. We worked with the U.S. Food & Drug Administration (FDA) throughout this episode to let the public know about this crime, and to protect our customers from this fake product.
>
> We are very happy to acknowledge that the FDA has apprehended one of the individuals believed to be responsible, and seized the manufacturing operations used in this illegal activity. The FDA reports

> that all known counterfeit product has been removed from retail stores. Parents can continue to use Similac products with full confidence.
>
> We have many people to thank for this successful outcome. First is the FDA, whose outstanding efforts brought about a swift conclusion. Second, are the many committed Abbott employees who worked round the clock, answering customer questions and assisting the FDA.
>
> Finally, and most importantly we want to thank you, our customer, for your continued trust and confidence in Similac.[1]

There are a number of positive things to be said of this letter, among them:

• It gives lots of information to all who read it: current customers of Similac; future customers; retailers, distributors, business partners, and even competitors.

• The tone is upbeat, reassuring, thankful, and positive. It conveys no evidence of malice toward the perpetrators (which might distract customers from the real message). More important, it doesn't seek to fix the blame anywhere else but where it belongs.

• The letter is careful not to go overboard in its sense of outrage at the people who attempted this crime. There is no whining, no finger-pointing, no sense that the company did not take complete control of the incident after it first surfaced. Readers of the letter can infer from its existence that the company was upset by the problem. But the organization carefully focuses the attention on the positive outcomes rather than on the negative ones.

• It makes significant, specific mention of its production and testing procedures as a way to demonstrate the company's constant and ongoing commitment to product quality control.

• It serves to distance the company and its product from the acts of the culprits and their counterfeit.

• It delivers plenty of praise exactly where it belongs: to FDA investigators; to Abbott Labs employees who, from this reading, appear to have worked extra hard to protect the company's name, reputation, and goodwill with their customers; and to its customers for sticking with the company through this tough time.

Overall, the text offers an excellent example of this paid-advertising, "open letter" public relations technique. Other companies, as we will see with Intel and its flawed computer chip, have not fared as well even after trying this approach. The Similac success story should serve as a positive example of how to communicate with the various audiences interested in a story and a product.

Tainted Food, Tainted Image: The Foodmaker Jack In The Box Case

It has been mighty hard sledding for Foodmaker, Inc., the San Diego–based parent company for the Jack In The Box fastfood chain. In January 1993, the hamburger restaurant fell prey to one of the worst product disasters imaginable: some of its meat became tainted by an outbreak of a deadly *E. coli* bacteria. In the end, three children died and 500 to 600 people became quite ill from eating bacteria-laden hamburgers made from this meat in some of its West Coast restaurants.

The majority of the stricken diners lived in the Washington State area, where two of the young children died. Other incidents occurred in California (where a little girl died north of San Diego), Oregon, and Nevada. The particular *E. coli* bacteria isolated in these tainted meat incidents was especially hard on small children, elderly people, and others with lowered immune systems.

Several lawsuits were filed: by lawyers on behalf of the sick and injured patrons; by nearly 100 angry franchisees who said that the parent company's mishandling of the incident almost drove them into bankruptcy; and by lawyers for the dead children and their families.

The financial impact on the company as a result of this

event was tremendous. And even at this printing, over three years after the outbreak, the company is still fighting to restore its image. A look at the numbers shows the hit the company took, right in its bottom line. By the end of fiscal year 1994, Foodmaker reported a $39.6 million loss—$6.1 in the final quarter alone. One business reporter called that figure the "good news," since the company had lost $98.1 million for the previous year. In fact, the company's last year of profitability prior to the incident was in 1992. Its stock, which had been as high as $10.87, fell in February 1995 to below the $4 mark. (And Foodmaker's first quarter 1995 report already showed a $20.5 million loss. While Foodmaker observers placed much of the blame for these heavy losses on the Jack In The Box tainted meat problem in 1993, the company is also heavily invested in a number of other money-losing restaurant chains not related to its hamburger stores.)

Let's Wait to Comment: Foodmaker's Early Media Response

Many of the details surrounding this event point to one key element: Hard though Foodmaker Jack In The Box tried to manage the crisis and handle the problems related to its image and the safety of its food, it simply did not do all it could have to protect its own interests, those of its franchisees, and most important, those of its current and future customers. Even people inside the company have quietly admitted to me that not only was the company caught off guard by the incident; it was unprepared for the emergency's scope and size. As a result, too much time elapsed before the company took significant steps to change its restaurant operating procedures or its handling of the information given to or uncovered by the media.

The Franchisees Swing in the Wind

From a business standpoint and from a public relations perspective, Jack In The Box did little to help its own cause with either the media *or* its franchisees, which for most fastfood companies are the lifeblood of success.

At this writing, there are approximately 1,231 Jack In The Box restaurants, including 816 company-owned stores and 415 operated by franchisees worldwide. In the summer following the outbreak, about 100 of these franchisees filed a class action suit against Foodmaker, claiming among other things a $100 million loss due to the problem.

Both sides had attempted to settle their financial differences during meetings between attorneys for the franchisees and Foodmaker, but they failed. In that respect, Foodmaker seemed to view its franchisees as adversaries and not as business partners. At one point, the franchisee association that initiated the suit against its parent asked the California State Department of Corporations to look into Foodmaker's "egregious and ongoing violations" of state franchise laws.

While both sides could and should have worked together to deal with their collective image problems, it appeared that since neither could settle the monetary issue, they drew apart and closed ranks. And by airing their dirty laundry in public, both sides—Foodmaker and its franchisees—continued to send out a message that said, in essence, "There are still plenty of problems around here!"

In September 1993, Foodmaker settled the case with its franchisees for $40.4 million. And to settle the more than 400 medical claims from sickened individual patrons in Washington state, Foodmaker created a $450,000 medical trust fund in Seattle to monitor the long-term health effects of those people who claimed to have gotten sick eating the tainted burgers. It also paid $1.3 million to settle the lawsuit for the family of a two-year-old boy who died in Tacoma, Washington, after eating a tainted cheeseburger. The lawsuit related to the death of the child in San Diego was also settled later for over $1 million.

No One Listens to "It's Not Our Fault"

Another participant in the case, and one that received surprisingly little media attention, was the tainted-meat *supplier,* grocery store giant Vons Company. Foodmaker had purchased the meat from Vons and yet, during the heat of the controversy, Vons's name was conspicuously absent from much of the media spotlight. Even the fact that Foodmaker sued Vons, its meat processor, and 10 other companies that provided the bad beef to Jack In The Box, received no more than a short mention in the newspapers.

Even today, it's puzzling why Vons and its meat-processing partners were not dragged through the mud like Foodmaker. Although Vons cautiously admitted providing the tainted meat, and therefore was at least partly responsible for the food-poisoning problem, at the start, why was it not held more culpable? Just in terms of "cause and effect," Foodmaker could have asked Vons to shoulder a more equal share of the public responsibility.

Yet in retrospect, trying to blame its meat provider would have probably proved to be a waste of time. The public that eats Jack In The Box hamburgers doesn't want to hear that; it wants to know when and if it's safe to go back to the restaurant or take their families there and eat the products.

Moreover, Vons could and did deflect initial criticism of its meat products by allowing suggestions to surface that Jack In The Box did not use approved health standards to process and cook the meat. Some critics argued that cooking the burger meat at a higher temperature would have killed most of the bacteria and made the meat safe to consume. It's hard to know if this might have prevented the problem.

The Hindsight View

To say that the *E. coli* bacteria breakout created a huge public relations mess for Foodmaker is like saying the Titanic ran into some difficulty with ice. From an examination of the press clippings and media interviews with various participants, victims, and attorneys involved in the case, and the messages sent by the top man, CEO Jack Goodall and his office, it's clear that the company was very unprepared for the crisis and simply reeled from one event to the next. Foodmaker needed to (and didn't) keep a weather eye on the various "publics" involved in this outbreak.

Each of the following groups had its own interest in the outcome of the event:

- Current Jack In The Box customers, who want to be reassured that this event was more of an aberration than a trend
- Potential Jack In The Box customers, who have either never eaten there or did in the past and now must consider whether or not to return
- Other (nonmeat) distributors who service Jack In The Box restaurant accounts, who wonder whether their products (French fries, buns, soda, etc.) will be tarred with the same "keep away, spoiled food" brush by consumers
- The franchisees, who responded in a predictable fashion when they felt the parent company had abandoned them and their needs
- Company stockholders and investors, who watched top management struggle with the crisis management issues and thereby helped drive the stock down to record lows
- The thousands of Jack In The Box restaurant employees and Foodmaker home office staffers who had to suffer under the same conditions as the top management

The employees surely had questions about the safety of the food along with the health and safety of their jobs. Companies don't take $40 million dollar hits without making staff cuts, and the employees may have felt just as confused as their customers. And from a personal point of view, it must have been difficult for many of the employees to admit to other people that they worked for a company involved in a tainted-food problem. The need to take pride in their work and in their employer must have made an already publicized event even more difficult.

Making It Right

Even Foodmaker admits that the cooking temperatures for its Jack In The Box restaurant grills were not as hot as they should have been. Again in hindsight, perhaps if they had not used the wrong temperature for their grills maybe no one would have been poisoned and it wouldn't have been a problem in the first place. Of course, the fact that the company started with tainted meat can't be ignored, but the grill temperature issue points to the hard-to-argue fact that Jack In The Box is the first major fastfood outfit in recent years whose customers have died after eating its food.

All this is not to say that Foodmaker and its restaurants intended for this to happen. Many of the executives, managers, and employees involved with the company felt heartbroken about what happened to the people who were sickened and the children who later died. No company should ever have to go through what Foodmaker did. But along with sympathy for the victims and survivors comes the need to look at past and present operations to ensure that something like this never happens again. Consider the fact that days passed before the company publicly announced it had changed its meat-cooking policies. By the time it got around to saying anything, the damage had been done, both to its reputation and to the level of prior consumer confidence.

What should the company have said? Here's a sample of one way it might first have expressed its regret and then demonstrated its willingness to institute immediate and sweeping changes in its food preparation policies:

> *Now that we've been alerted to this problem, we've immediately recalibrated every one of our grills in every one of our restaurants. We've also retrained every one of our restaurant managers and employees as to these new standards. We want to make sure that the aberration that occurred at one group of our restaurants will never happen anywhere again.*

Will people feel better if you deny or downplay the event and thereby create the message, however subtly, that they may be harmed if they use or consume one of your products? Or will they feel reassured if you tell them the immediate steps you have taken or will take?

How would *you* react to these conflicting messages: one that says, "It's not our fault and oh, by the way, it's safe to eat our food," or one that states, "We've taken steps to ensure that our grills are hotter, our meat is better inspected, and our cooking procedures are now higher than industry standards"?

And to take the hindsight concept even further, consider the impact on its bottom line if Foodmaker had closed every one of its restaurants for one whole day and given every employee new and updated training in better food handling procedures. (In military parlance, this "stop for safety" operation is known as a stand-down. Here, policies and procedures, tools and operations, and training and personnel are given a thorough inspection by the workers and leaders.)

Would it have cost Foodmaker Jack In The Box $40 million to retrain all the employees in its 1,200-plus stores? Since the crystal ball is still in the shop for repairs, we can only speculate how differently all this might have turned out had Foodmaker taken a more proactive training stance long before any deadly *E. coli* bacteria ever arrived on its hamburger meat.

Consider your own options if this problem arose at your restaurant, food supply warehouse, or food manufacturing plant. What might you want to do? Stay open and ride it out or close for one day of stand-down retraining time? Might you want to:

- Consider shutting down the operation, plant, facility, or restaurant for at least one day while you publicly investigated the causes of the problem?
- Immediately institute an on-the-spot retraining procedure? You could create an in-house video tape program to demonstrate the proper cooking or food handling procedures and then ship the copies by overnight mail to all your franchise restaurants, chains, or branch facilities.
- Go to the public and to the media with these changes, not in days or weeks, but within *hours?*

> In times like this—especially when young kids have died as a result of eating your product—the CEO or other senior company leader must bear the yoke of responsibility.

Yes, it's true that Foodmaker CEO Jack Goodall did not personally handle the meat or make the hamburgers, but as the figurehead for the company, he was expected, by his customers and other observers, to shoulder the blame, absorb the predictable slings and arrows, and go about explaining how and why this event would never, ever happen to Jack In The Box again.

The company's use of the media was more reactive than proactive; the CEO did not come forward immediately as the spokesman for the problem. The parent company spent months after the incident fighting its way through lawsuits that merely dredged up the ineptitudes that had followed the first notice of the problem.

For its part, the company did do the right thing by quickly settling the death cases with the families and by establishing the medical trust fund to care for the longterm health of some of the victims.

But in terms of all these dollar-choking lawsuits, suppose Jack Goodall had gone to the microphone and said, "We're very concerned about the health and welfare of our customers who came across this isolated batch of bad meat. We expect to do our part to compensate them for this incident. As such, we will settle every bona fide case of exposure to the *E. coli* bacteria, no questions asked." Surely Foodmaker's attorneys would have screamed in pain and never let him say that, least of all in public. But after paying out $40 million to various litigants, how could it have been any worse?

No Rebound in Sight: Foodmaker Jumps Back Into the Fire

And the beat goes on for Foodmaker. It 1995 ad campaign heralding the return of its corporate clown's-head logo (literally blown up and destroyed by a bomb in TV commercials in 1980) could not have come at a worse time for them. It features the new Jack (a man in a suit wearing a big clown's head), blowing up the boardroom filled with his current bosses. The message for the commercial was supposed to be: "Jack's back." Instead, it brought howls of protest from advertising and consumer groups who believe that anything glorifying bombings—in this era of workplace violence, the Unabomber, and the attacks on the World Trade Center and the Oklahoma federal building—is in incredibly poor taste.

The ad was created by Foodmaker and ad king Chiat/Day, who together in a statement said, "We discussed the violent content of the ad and thought few people would take it seriously."

The editors at *TV Guide,* no strangers to tasteless commercials, had this to say about it:

> Jeers to the commercial for the [Jack In The Box] burger chain that showed a mad bomber in a clown costume blowing up the company's board of directors. It was *supposed* to be funny—the clown himself was blown up in an ad 15 years ago, and this was his comic "revenge." Unfortunately, the spot ran during a period when a New Jersey ad exec was killed by a mail bomb, an explosive went off in a New York City subway and terrorists tried to blow up a plane over Paris. Our beef is not [just] with the bad timing, but with the company's reluctance to pull the ad off the box.[2]

By the end of the Foodmaker meat problem, three children had died, several hundred people had gotten extremely sick, and a parent company with a previously long history of success (the first Jack In The Box opened in the early 1960s) had to learn an expensive, painful lesson in how *not* to manage a real crisis event.

Only time and the natural ebb and flow of consumer forgetfulness will help Foodmaker and its Jack In The Box restaurants finally distance themselves from this tragedy. Foodmaker had little choice but to pay the money to the survivors and franchisees and try to move on. As its current financial condition indicates, the recovery will continue to be slow.

Bogus Product Tampering: Pepsi Takes an Aggressive Stance

In the 1983 movie *Strange Brew,* Dave Thomas and Rick Moranis star as two beer-swilling Canadians known as the McKenzie Brothers. In a classic product-tampering scene, they decide to take a baby mouse, insert it carefully into an empty beer bottle and then feed and care for it for several weeks until it's fully grown and now stuck inside the bottle. Then they pour some beer back into the bottle, drive to their local brewery with the beer-trapped mouse in tow, and demand free beer for life.

This idea or ones like it have not been lost over the years on money-hungry scam artists posing as innocent consumers. And life does occasionally imitate art, as Pepsi-Cola found out in early June 1993, when the first reports began to surface in Tacoma, Washington, and New Orleans about syringes found inside cans of Pepsi. By June 23, 1993, more than 50 people from dozens of states had come forward and said that they too had found foreign objects—needles, screws, pins, syringes—in their cans of Pepsi.

And so began the Great Pepsi Scare of 1993. Even the FDA got into the act. According to a *BusinessWeek* article that ran one month later, Pepsi-Cola North America CEO Craig E. Weatherup was in the backyard of his home one weekend when the phone rang (remember again that all bad phone calls related to your business come on weekends or in the wee hours of the morning):

> I got a call from the commissioner of the FDA. I'd never met [Commissioner] David Kessler or talked to him, but it was clear we knew the same thing: that for this to be happening defied logic.[3]

And yet it *was* happening, and within days, Weatherup, as a *Time* Magazine piece put it, "scurried from *Nightline* to *MacNeil/Lehrer* to the morning network shows, looking concerned and attempting damage control."[4]

And as difficult as it may have been to go on network television six times and repeat his request not to boycott his product on the grounds of safety, Weatherup made his point. And in a classic, bring-it-to-them-first move, a Pepsi video team shot footage of the canning production process and showed the public that it would be nearly physically impossible to put syringes into the cans. (The cans move at extremely high speeds and it would take nothing short of a complete assembly line stoppage to get any item, much less a syringe, into one can.)

Some media types, including Ted Koppel, were calling on Pepsi and Weatherup to pull the product from the store shelves—no small feat considering the number of cans that sit at any one time in every grocery, liquor, and convenience store on the planet. Weatherup decided that rather than attempt a recall, his company would advise people to put their sodas into glasses before drinking them, at least until they got to the bottom of the so-called "syringe scare."

By the time of Weatherup's *Nightline* appearance, in which Weatherup had FDA Commissioner David Kessler firmly in support of Pepsi, the police were already starting to make arrests for filing false injury claims. Soon the scams came crashing down as law enforcement, health officials, and other investigators began to uncover case after case of bogus tampering claims, all aimed at extracting cash from the giant soda maker.

And while the FDA was announcing that the cases they had investigated were hoaxes, Pepsi and Weatherup continued to work hard to reassure their bottlers, distributors, and consumers that their products were safe, drinkable, and free from anything other than soda water, bubbles, and syrup.

By the end of June, the FBI had made 20 arrests and they and the FDA were unable to find a single substantiated case of product tampering by Pepsi or anyone else not in it for the money or their 15 minutes of TV news fame.

Weatherup defended his decision not to recall his products. He agreed that if legitimate consumers had been injured, poisoned, or killed, it would have been a different story. And even after Pepsi knew that the claims had finally been put down as frauds, ripoffs, scams, and hoaxes, Weatherup ordered full-page ads in 12 national papers, and his bottlers ran similar ads in 300 to 400 local papers. As the *Time* Magazine piece put it, "Pepsi found itself at the center of one of the weirdest such ripples of the media age, first as alleged victimizer, then as stoic victim."[5] In retrospect, the latter role is not such a bad one to play; it's always easier to be outraged when the facts and the evidence are on your side.

Going on the Offensive and the Defensive

It's clear from a review of the facts surrounding the bogus Pepsi-tampering incidents that the vast majority of them were scams created by unscrupulous people with two goals in mind: first, to make a big company sweat and second, to try and get some money out of it. There were some cases that could not be proved either way and may have been the result of some mistake by the consumer of the product. But the boycott threat was largely from less-than-honorable consumers who saw a chance to score when the initial case broke and then improvised with their own opportunities. For their part, both Pepsi as a company and Craig Weatherup as its CEO were too bright for these people, some of whom were caught on grocery store video security cameras adding metal parts to cans they had just opened.

For its part, the media seemed to share the first goals with the opportunistic hoax victims; in their fervor to put the new story on the air, they fed into the "Pull the product from the store shelves before it kills somebody" angle.

The press wanted to put Pepsi through its paces as well and see how it responded to increasing public and media pressure to take bold steps. Just ask Craig Weatherup (who worked 20-hour days during the height of the crisis) if he enjoyed going on television and repeating the same message—"Our products are safe"—over and over while newscasters and TV hosts asked him when he planned to recall every can Pepsi had made since the founding of the company.

An important question arises from all this: Did Pepsi overreact at the start? Might it have been better served to wait, gather more information, and then move ahead with more specific actions later?

Did the company really believe its customers would think Pepsi cans were actually coming off the assembly line with syringes or metal parts in them? Perhaps this points out the need to step back and take a 360-degree, helicopter view of the problem at hand. Maybe your first, gut-level response is not your wisest one.

Back in hindsight, we can now see that one crackpot and

another dozen opportunists does not a crisis make. When the greedy copycats got in over their heads and couldn't effectively explain to the police or FDA investigators how their specific syringe got into their specific soda can, their claims tumbled rather quickly.

But Pepsi had several distinct advantages over firms like Foodmaker, Johnson & Johnson, Perrier (they of the Benzene-tainted designer water problem) and other firms who really *did* have bad things happen to their products. For one, Pepsi knew it hadn't done anything that would have allowed foreign objects to get into its cans. For another, it knew it had already done everything during production to *prevent* this kind of problem from ever happening in the first place. And finally, it was ready with something TV news people always want, videotape—in this case, videotape that showed the whole Pepsi creation process.

Weatherup knew the firm had so many quality controls, tests, product reviews and samplings, that tampering would be nearly impossible. He was able to convince the public to back his product by letting the media carry his message for him. His efforts and the efforts of his company calmed nervous consumers and swung public confidence back over to Pepsi.

For his part, Craig Weatherup walked his talk and talked his walk. He served as the point man for the media, not just for his boss, PepsiCo Inc. Chairman D. Wayne Calloway. He deserves credit for sticking to his message—"Our product is safe and we won't recall it"—from start to finish.

And to return to the subject of the McKenzie brothers and their movie, a female attorney from Somers, New York, was convicted by a federal jury of trying to blackmail Pepsi-Cola for damages and for filing a false claim with the FDA. In the April 1994 conviction, the jury found that the 38-year-old woman was threatening to sue Pepsi-Cola on the false grounds that she found a dead mouse in her can of Caffeine Free Diet Pepsi unless the company settled with her for her pain and suffering and other psychological damages.

This incident took place almost one year after the Pepsi syringe scare.

The Intel Pentium Flaw: First It Wasn't One, Then It Was

The good news is that Intel Corporation is the galaxy's leading manufacturer of computer chips. It's the world's largest semiconductor company and the first one ever to sell more than $10 billion in products. Intel processors run 8 out of every 10 computers sold in the world. Motorola, its closest competitor, sells fewer than 1 in 10.

The bad news is that, in its first issue of the 1995 new year, *BusinessWeek* listed Intel's problems with its acclaimed Pentium chip as the second "Dumbest Move of 1994." To quote from the list:

> Its Pentium chip flawed, Intel treated worried customers with arrogance. It waited six months after finding the glitch before offering replacements to any who asked.[6]

But before you shed any tears for Intel, consider that even after taking a *$475 million* pretax charge in its 1994 fourth quarter to replace or write off its flawed Pentium chip, it's still an $11.5 billion company. Intel also managed to squeak out a mere $2.3 billion net. First-quarter 1995 profits were a scant $889 million.

Is the lesson here that if you're big enough, have lots of cash, brand name recognition, and leading market share position, you can screw up your image and still recover? In a word, yes.

Had this same product reliability problem happened to a smaller, upstart, or struggling computer firm, could it have weathered the publicity storm that followed? Could it have offered a response to its customers that Intel's own CEO Andrew Grove later apologetically admitted was "arrogant and uncaring"? It's doubtful, especially since, in everything from guns and schoolyard bullies to football players and skyscrapers, size counts, big is best, and those with the most resources (read that as actual cash) can usually outlast their competitors or critics.

The background for this hubbub began after Intel released

its Pentium chip in March 1993 and later spent $150 million to advertise it on television. Intel had quite an investment in the success of the product, and clearly, this media blitz paid off. Even the average computer user or buyer, who wouldn't usually know a microchip from a chocolate chip, could point to his or her new computers and tell colleagues, friends, and co-workers about the virtues of "Intel Inside" the box. In short, Intel's name recognition ad campaign worked well and continues to work, despite the initial impact of the Pentium flaw.

Public awareness began after the publication on December 21, 1994 of a *USA Today* piece, which suggested that Intel had poorly managed the complaints of a math professor from Lynchburg College in Virginia who had discovered a processing flaw six months earlier when he asked his computer to conquer some highly complicated math problems.

When the professor received no help from Intel technical support staffers in October 1994, he contacted colleagues, and soon the story ended up on the Internet. Within days, Internet users and other on-line members got caught up in the story and it began to take on a life of its own.

November and December 1994 were hard months for Intel and Grove. The company set up a separate 800 number to deal with the rising number of questions and complaints about the chip from anxious computer customers. And though Grove did meet with his top executives on Thanksgiving Day to map out a response to the growing controversy (the "it happens-over-a-holiday" theme rides again), the company stuck to its party line which said in essence, "We don't believe the flaw is significant enough to worry about. Our tests show it would create a wrong answer every 27,000 years. Therefore, don't call us about it, we'll call you if we discover it's serious."

However, other testers came up with many wrong answers, including IBM, Intel's biggest customer. IBM said its test operations showed that the chip would create an error every 20 days.

Not only did Intel not admit that the flaw was of any consequence, it continued to insist that frustrated users prove why they needed a new chip. This only added to consumers' miseries, and not just those of sophisticated computer programmers and designers who used the chip to perform intense calculations. It also was upsetting to average users who knew only that their machines had some kind of problem and that it might flair up and ruin their next big proposal, sales report, Great American Novel, or customer spreadsheet.

In mid-December 1994, IBM backed up its concern by refusing to ship any of its PCs with Pentium chips inside them. Here was a huge computer company, IBM, going head-to-head with its biggest supplier, Intel, and telling it: "Either you get your act together, correct the product, and offer free replacements or we will take our (substantial) business elsewhere."

At this point, Intel's stock immediately fell 2 percent and, for a brief period, trading was temporarily suspended. IBM succeeded in doing what Intel customers could not; in effect, getting it to reverse course. By the end of that month, Intel hoisted a white flag and agreed to make immediate and free exchanges of the chip for anyone who requested it. The company set up another product replacement telephone hotline and authorized its dealers and distributors to make the repairs at Intel's cost, which some analysts suggest will cost them about $100 per computer. (Multiply that by the estimated 2.2 million chips in use today, and it's no small flaw. Not everyone will bother to exchange their chip, however, since it seems only to fail during the more sophisticated type of operations that many business people just don't do. But for those who might think this chip is waiting to fail with each tick of the clock, the replacement service is a welcome and necessary peace-of-mind builder.)

The Stonewall Approach Fails

As you will see in Chapter 4's discussion of the Los Angeles Police Department and its handling of both the Rodney King video incident and the subsequent riots that followed, there is no public patience today for organizations and leaders who try to avoid an obvious problem by ignoring it, passing the buck, or otherwise trying to convince the public that they are not wrong when they are.

Customers tried and often failed to get Intel to listen to their pleas for help. The company was slow to respond and tried to explain away valid concerns about errors as a "nine-billion-to-one chance." In some respects this smacks of intellectual arrogance and the use of technical "superiority" over Intel's customers, many of whom are actually extremely sharp. Intel also failed to respect the fact that, unlike industries in which change is more gradual, the computer field reinvents itself just about overnight. Intel did not understand that the computer marketplace is driven by people who talk constantly to each other about their new machines, software, problems, and potential solutions, *and* about their constant search for newer, faster, and better machinery, technology, and self-knowledge. To think that people who rap on their respective keyboards with such fervor would not demand satisfaction and new chips is amazingly shortsighted.

Only after IBM held Intel's feet to the fire did Intel agree to make the appropriate, timely, and necessary changes. And this sent yet another message to their customers, which was: "We'll wait until this chip flaw hits us more directly in our pocketbook (IBM's future business) before we respond to you. It will take one of our significant business partners, not our customers at large, to get us to move."

One *BusinessWeek* reader wrote to the magazine with his reaction to Intel's less-than-straightforward handling of the Pentium chip flaw. Leon Reinstein from Baltimore, Maryland had this to say:

> Future generations of business school students will study Intel Corp.'s response to the problems with the Pentium chip as a classic case study in how to transform a technical problem into a public-relations nightmare.
>
> Intel's five-point plan consisted of:
>
> 1. Initially deny that the problem exists;
> 2. When irrefutable evidence is presented that the problem exists, downplay its significance;

3. Agree to only replace items for people who can demonstrate extreme hardship;
4. Continue running your current ad campaign extolling the virtues of the product as if nothing has happened;
5. Count the short-term profits.[7]

His sentiments matched those of other Intel computer users who have been just as vocal in their complaints, apprehensions, and concerns that without intervention from a higher authority (Big Blue), the rank-and-file paying customers would still not have received any satisfaction.

With Abbot Labs' Similac open letter in mind, and Pepsi's own public run of reassurance letters following its syringe scare, here's the full-page, nationally run effort finally offered on December 21, 1994, by Intel's President and CEO Andrew Grove, Executive Vice President and Chief Operating Officer Craig Barrett, and Chairman of the Board Gordon Moore:

> To owners of Pentium processor-based computers and the PC community:
>
> We at Intel wish to sincerely apologize for our handling of the recently publicized Pentium processor flaw.
>
> The Intel Inside® symbol means that your computer has a microprocessor second to none in quality and performance.
>
> Thousands of Intel employees work very hard to ensure that this is true. But no microprocessor is ever perfect.
>
> What Intel continues to believe is technically an extremely minor problem has taken on a life of its own. Although Intel firmly stands behind the quality of the current version of the Pentium processor, we recognize that many users have concerns.
>
> We want to resolve those concerns.

> Intel will exchange the current version of the Pentium processor for an update version, in which this floating-point divide flaw is corrected, for any owner who requests it, free of charge anytime during the life of their computer.[8]

While almost any public statement like this is better than nothing, the letter misses the mark on several points. For one, it still oozes intellectual arrogance and technical superiority. Where is the nontechnical definition (or even any previous mention) of the "floating-point divide flaw"? How many customers who are not computer, software, or electrical engineers would even know what this means?

Compare this missive with the Similac example and note that the Intel letter, while informative, lacks personality or the human touch. People don't want to hear that "no microprocessor is ever perfect" from the company that just sold them a microprocessor. Most folks—even those with no technical background—are smart enough to realize that machines are fallible and that no chip is ever going to be error-free. But the message that should have come from Intel was, "We are sorry for any *inconvenience* this incident caused for *you,* our customers." Frankly speaking, that the problem had "taken on a life of its own" was no one's fault but Intel's. The company should have reassured its customers early and often that it would replace the chip if that's what they wanted. Certainly not every Pentium chip buyer would have taken up Intel's offer, but the positive significance of such a responsive public gesture would not have been missed.

Sophisticated business computer users might only call on their machines for word processing functions, mailing list management, sales record keeping, and basic accounting functions. Most basic business users might need only two or three functions from the above list. Few of us have the desire, energy, or need to run complex mathematical algorithms, write our own software code, or place such demands on the Pentium that it might fail or create errors.

But the more Intel denied the existence of the flaw, the more average computer users worried that their machine would suddenly crash in the middle of their next important project. It simply makes sense; if you never give your computer chip much thought, only a controversy from the manufacturer could force your attention back to the essential viability of the machine. By not acting swiftly, Intel *created* apprehension in its customers that might not otherwise have arisen.

Lessons Learned: Be Proactive and Reactive

These four cases of product problems are not the only ones that have ever occurred. They are just more noticeable because of the size of the companies at which they happened and the massive amounts of publicity that surrounded each one.

In retrospect, the makers of Similac and Pepsi-Cola took charge of their respective situations early and forcefully. They handled their respective publics—their customers, consumers, distributors, business partners, and shareholders—as well as they managed the media. They made unswerving efforts to get to the bottom of their problems and apologized for any inconvenience or apprehension the incidents caused.

Further, there was no evidence of blame or excuse-making within the organization or to the world at large. These companies understood the simple fact that people who are not on the inside (read that as customers and the media) want to know the real facts and hear the truth as early as possible.

In contrast, Foodmaker and Intel, both large and successful enough to know better, did not appear to have control over their respective incidents. They let events and incoming problems manage *them* rather than the reverse. They did not take immediate steps to communicate with their publics either quickly or on a regular basis. Many of their customers were left in the dark and felt understandably apprehensive. Both companies seemed to see the media as more of a hindrance than a help, and adopted a "Don't call us, we'll call you" stance in the face of many hard questions from the press.

For Foodmaker's leaders, much of the time following the painful announcements of sickness and death from *E. coli* was spent circling the wagons and attempting to handle internal, private problems (with suppliers, individual restaurants, etc.) rather than the external ones. Initial public statements to create confidence in the firm's subsequent action steps were notable for their absence.

In the Intel situation, since news and business reporters weren't getting much information from the company's key executives, they went elsewhere for comments—to competing computer companies, salespeople, disgruntled customers, online service enthusiasts, stock market analysts, and other folks who, while they had valid opinions, were certainly not speaking for Intel. The *company leaders,* as Intel finally realized, should have spoken up for their company.

Notes

1. Copyright Abbott Labs, "An Open Letter From the Makers of Similac®," February 14, 1995.
2. "Cheers 'N' Jeers," *TV Guide,* January 14, 1995.
3. Zinn, Laura, "The Right Moves, Baby," *BusinessWeek,* July 5, 1993, pp. 30–31.
4. Toufexis, Anastasia, "A Weird Case, Baby? Uh Huh!," *Time,* June 28, 1993, p. 41.
5. Ibid.
6. "UpFront—Dumbest Moves of 1994," *BusinessWeek,* January 9, 1995.
7. Letters to the Editor, *BusinessWeek,* January, 25, 1995, p. 13.
8. Copyright Intel, "To Pentium Owners" letter, December 21, 1994.

4

Image Disasters

The biggest liar in the world is "They say."

—Douglas Malloch

What follows is a veritable rogue's gallery of modern-day corporate image crises. Some were created by the organization's own inability to see the big picture, some by outsiders with their own agendas, and some by internal or external forces that inadvertently sent the company spinning in the wrong direction. These cases involve well-known companies and their leaders. In each instance, the image problem started insignificantly enough, then grew to resemble large quicksand pits bordered by puddles of tar.

As with the previous chapter, which focused on specific product problems, these image nightmares focus on various things that went wrong and right, and why. For every mistake, bad decision, or incorrect choice, there are also examples of good ideas, positive solutions, and innovative management thinking that came from flexible, aware, and prepared company leaders.

An Oldie but Goodie: Satanism at Procter & Gamble

For what seems now like all eternity, the home products giant Procter & Gamble has had to fight the fifteen-year-old rumor that its company logo represents Satan or some sort of devil-worshiping event. What looks like stars and the moon to most people has taken on satanic overtones to certain individuals with too much free time, stern-faced religious groups, and other people who see things that go bump in the night.

This odd controversy has continued since 1980 in one form or another, and it seems to get brought up in even the most generic business articles about P&G. As such, when it gets mentioned in passing, it's almost as if this image problem were a part of the firm's corporate history. Business school textbooks about public relations, marketing, and image management have mentioned it, used it as a case study, and otherwise kept the fires burning under it long after the issue should have died a natural death.

While it's hard now (or even when the rumor first touched our national consciousness) to believe that a hundred-year-old company would actually choose a logo with even a hint of the Devil in it, the rumor continues to resurface, and these two forces—P&G and Beelzebub—somehow carom off each other in the press. Just as Kentucky Fried Chicken faces the occasional "fried rats in the chicken" rumor, Procter & Gamble seems destined to ride this one out for a few more years.

The story has become part of the way some people still think about P&G, even when they don't believe that it's entirely true. The majority of consumers have absolutely no qualms about using the company's products, think the logo looks harmless, and put no stock in the rumor. Yet somehow, the same people go on remembering P&G's logo controversy; they heard the rumor when it first surfaced and it sticks with them.

Has this problem hurt P&G's overall success? No, not unless you count billions in sales as bad. Yet, by the same yardstick, the firm has had to spend millions on advertisements, court costs, and associated public relations bills to categorically deny the charge. At one point, when the rumor started up once again in August 1995, the company was answering nearly 200 phone calls a day from confused consumers who had heard various spurious rumors that P&G's president was going to give a "large portion of profits to his satanic church."

In one case, in 1991, the company successfully sued a Parsons, Kansas, couple for $75,000. It seems that this husband and wife were the local Amway distributors for their area, and had restarted the Satan-worship rumor as a way to help the sales of their own competing cleaning products.

Procter & Gamble filed another Amway-derived suit in August 1995 against Randy L. Haugen, an independent Amway distributor from Ogden, Utah, who, according to court records, made false and defamatory statements about P&G's link to satanism. This marks the sixth suit filed against Amway or an Amway distributor and the fifteenth the company has had to file to protect its image since this controversy began in 1980.

For the sake of discussion, let's say that the same controversy were announced today, as a brand-new image problem. What alternatives, assets, or approaches does the company have now that it might not have had access to 15 years ago? Consider the following corporate self-defense options:

• *Use the presence of instant, widespread, mainstream media coverage to refute the claim.* This can be both a positive and a negative, but the fact that there are so many more information channels today suggests that companies can now fight their battles in the open and come out on top if the public believes them from the outset.

A story like P&G's, with its built-in "You must be joking!" factor already in place, affords the company the superior position—that is, *if* it takes to the truth-toting high ground and explains its position clearly, quickly, and without the slightest hint of evasion. But as we have seen from the previous chapter, that can be a mighty big *if*. Faced with a similar problem, other companies have stonewalled the story so much at the onset that it soon takes on a life of its own.

The value of so much press coverage—or more important, access—lies in its instantaneous exposure to a wide audience. Use it or lose it; now is the best time to put a halt to the rumor since your chances of total eradication diminish with time.

• *Take a sniper approach to the problem.* This means take one shot, make one kill, leave it for dead, and move on. Here again, the way the company handles time can be a critical success factor. The leaders of any organization (especially one as large as P&G) should be able to direct the appropriate corporate spokespeople to create a national press release within *hours* of the first sign of this kind of brewing trouble.

Hitting an emerging image problem hard and fast can take the wind out of its sails. As media and public relations expert Chet Burchett will explain in Chapters 7 and 8, the faster you can assist the media and the faster they in turn realize (through your education process) that it is a nonissue, the faster it will end.

• *Take the blitz approach to the problem.* In other words, throw money at it hard and fast, until the most vocal critics run out of energy, motivation, or cash. If you've got the cash to do it, you can set a lot of your executives, department heads, managers, employees, and outside experts into motion.

Another possibility is to throw lawyers and the real possibility of civil suits at the instigators and threaten their financial well-being with the promise of a court date. Sometimes if you attack the most vocal critics or hidden agenda-ists with a campaign of your own, you can exhaust them long before they ever get to you.

The blitz approach calls for certainty of purpose, knowledge of prior plans, and a lightning response. (And, frankly, it requires a tinge of ruthlessness that says, "Nobody is going to create false stories about our company without seeing us rattle our sabres.") Don't let even one week go by before acting on a bona fide assault on your image.

• *Fight back in a humorous, memorable, or otherwise extreme manner designed to weaken your attackers and show your various publics how ridiculous the whole thing is.* Think outside the usual stiff-upper-lip, button-down mind-set for a moment. Why not be just as outrageous as the claims made against you? What would have happened if the Procter & Gamble spokesperson had come out to address a room crowded with reporters, all the while wearing a red cape across the back of his business suit, a plastic pair of red devil horns on his head, and a red plastic pitchfork in his hand? First, every jaw in the place would have dropped a foot. And second, you wouldn't have been able to hear over the din of laughter and "What gives?" questions that would have followed.

And what would have been the public's reaction if P&G had gotten a few hundred of their employees to wear discount-store devil Halloween costumes to work the next day? Even their staunchest critics would have had to admit secretly, "You know, this whole Satan-logo thing is dumb. We didn't really believe that stuff in the first place." And as for the rest of the buying public, they'd probably have gotten as huge a kick out of it as the employees.

The message here is "We work hard around here, but we also know when it's time to have a little fun. When some person or some group makes this kind of utterly outrageous claim, we can't help but get our creative juices flowing and think up a truly goofy way to respond in kind." Where is the harm in showing the world that your organization is not just a faceless amalgamated giant, but a group of people bent on doing the best job they can for their customers?

In recent years, shoemaker Thom McAn, a company founded in 1922, found itself with flagging shoe sales and a stodgy, humorless look. A small ad agency created a new campaign for the firm that focused on poking fun at itself. Speaking of its reputation for out-of-date shoe styles, one ad read, "Through a fluke computer error, the office supply store sent us the wrong desk calendars and we thought it was still 1976." Says Nick Cohen, whose agency created the series of spots, "You have to use a bit of self-deprecation to get people to take you seriously."[1]

Granted, most public relations experts, mainstream ad writers, or nervous attorneys would just as soon eat their briefcases as suggest such an outrageous idea, but you must admit that fighting stupid with stupid has its merits.

The key to fighting back with humor or some other memorable tactic lies in the public's and the media's perception of your corporate image in the first place. It may be one thing for the folks at Ben & Jerry's to poke fun at themselves; it's quite another for the operators of a nuclear power plant to suggest that spontaneous and uncontrolled frivolity are the usual order of the day. Some things require a staid approach, while others, like Satan in the washing powder, call for a more sublime one.

For its part, Procter & Gamble will certainly continue along as it always has—like a venerable, veteran, market share giant, lead-holding business with a long history of success and not much time for that tiny percentage of our population that seeks to find something wrong with everything. It's unfortunate that the company has had to waste its time, money, and energy fighting an image problem no intelligent person really thinks much about anyway. But as the "Age of the Need For the Carefully Selected Soundbite" continues to prove, our society expects answers.

Still Made From the Best Stuff on Earth: Snapple Fights Back

Snapple Beverages is a Valley Stream, New York, maker of teas and sweet drinks that ships about 90 million cases of these products to retailers and distributors every year. It has seen good product placement on such diversely entertaining shows as *Seinfeld* and the trashy but popular Howard Stern radio and TV programs.

In September 1993, Snapple leaders found themselves trapped in the uncomfortable glare of the media spotlight. Rumors began to circulate in San Francisco and other West Coast cities that the kosher food K on the Snapple label was some kind of symbol for the Ku Klux Klan. Worse yet, other race baiters and hate peddlers believed that the Snapple label, which actually depicts the Boston Tea Party, seemed to show black slaves on ships.

Snapple was forced to take out large newspaper ads in many cities to dispel these myths. As company president Leonard March put it:

> The rumors were so ridiculous we thought they would go away, but they didn't. It reached the point it was getting out of hand and we had to address it.[2]

The perception of Snapple has always been of a good-tasting, attractively-packaged bottle of tea or juice. So to think that the company would get blindsided by a rumor of racism is hard to fathom. The company was founded, as they like to put it, "by three Jewish boys from Brooklyn," so any claims of either anti-Semitism or KKK affiliation just don't take into account who's running things over at Snapple.

To its credit, once Snapple executives decided to fight off the rumor with a publicity campaign of their own, they wasted no time in squelching the racism claim. The firm took out advertisements in papers like the *San Francisco Chronicle* and the *Oakland Tribune,* and ran clarification ads on a number of Bay Area radio stations as part of a week-long attack on the problem.

In retrospect, the firm's leaders can argue that the money was well spent, especially in light of the issue at hand: race relations and the real possibility of a history-making scandal or boycott attached forever like glue to the product. While it must have been hard to spend good money on such a specious claim, the Snapple executives probably realized early on that they should attack the problem while it was largely confined to one geographic area.

Speaking of Snapple's quandary as to whether to ignore the rumor or spend the money to fight it, one securities analyst for Paine Webber said:

> This kind of thing can hurt sales if it gets out of hand. If you say nothing, consumers have no reason to think the rumor is not true.[3]

The old saying, "If it's bad, it happens, and if it's good, it goes away," applies here. Armed with the knowledge that this issue was not about to dry up on its own, Snapple executives initiated image protection plans, took the right steps, and quashed the rumor with some effective damage control moves and information-based advertising.

What would you do if your product or service were linked to a racial problem? How might you defend your firm from false pronouncements that made people believe you were biased, bigoted, or otherwise insensitive to any member of the so-called protected classes—i.e., women, minorities, the disabled, gays, or the elderly? With diversity, equal employment requirements, and the desire to right past wrongs in terms of equal treatment of these groups, you might consider the following bold steps to protect your image from this taint:

• *Initiate an immediate and thorough audit of your organization, its products, and services, to see if any racially driven claims are remotely possible or actually true.* Sometimes we don't see the forest because all those trees happen to be in the way. It's easy to get so caught up in the designing, marketing, and selling of your products or services that you forget about the impact these processes may have on certain groups of people.

The leaders at Snapple asked themselves a hard question, "Is it at all possible to construe the information and design of our product label as being racist or otherwise offensive to minority groups?"

Their answer was an immediate no, which they followed with an explanation campaign designed to educate everyone about why the label looked as it did.

These types of questions are not easy to ask, but they are essential to your company's ongoing assessment. And instead of asking yourself, "Gee, I wonder if group X would find this product, policy, or circumstance offensive?" you need to find people from that minority group or protected class and ask *them* for their opinions. These times call for sensitive handling of these issues. You must address any possible discrepancies as valid, especially if someone has already started the process for you.

• *Contact bona fide representatives of the groups by letter, then by phone if possible.* See if they will discuss their findings with you and allow you to discuss yours with them. If appropriate, ask them to come to your facility to meet you and see what's going on for themselves.

As we will see in the next chapter, this worked for the Denny's restaurant chain after it was found to have violated discrimination laws with respect to the seating and service of black patrons. Company leaders made sweeping changes in Denny's policies and worked hand-in-hand with the NAACP to increase the number of minority-owned restaurants.

• *If you have been publicly called to task on racial or gender questions, work to sell your position by notifying the press of your findings, communications with groups or representatives, and any other attempts to solve the problem amicably.* If your company suddenly becomes embroiled in a controversy surrounding uneven or unfair racial, gender, or ADA (Americans with Disabilities Act)-related treatment of employees or customers, you can bet the news media will find out about it first from them, and only second from you. And once the event becomes news, it can be hard to change the media's and the public's initial impressions that your firm is discriminatory in its policies or operations.

If you've taken bold steps or admitted to some past problems in your hiring policies or sales or service practices, communicate those messages, first to the people involved and then to the media. You want to demonstrate that you're trying to solve these kinds of problems, not run from them. Keeping everything hush-hush and under wraps until some future date (or *always* behind closed doors) will only convince the media that you are not being truthful, ethical, or forthright in the way you've chosen to handle the problem. Use the media as a conduit to get information to the various people and groups who are watching you.

• *Notify your employees about possible changes, announcements, or other actions that they may have heard about or that may affect them.* It's easy to get so caught up in a potential or a fully engulfing controversy regarding your organization that you forget about the people below top management level: your employees. They probably know more about what's going on than you think. They read newspapers, watch TV newscasts, and more important, talk with their customers and amongst themselves up and down the company chain of command or grapevine.

If you plan to make sweeping changes—i.e., create a mentoring program for minority employees or remove, add, or change hiring policies designed to reflect increased diversity sensitivity—don't let them be the last to know about it.

Extra Oil at Exxon

It's hard to add much to the facts most people already know about the Exxon oil spill. On March 24, 1989, the Exxon *Valdez* oil tanker ran aground in Alaska's Prince William Sound and dumped upwards of 11 million gallons of oil into the water and onto the shorelines of the area.

From a bottom-line standpoint, this accident has forced Exxon to spend an estimated $2.1 billion in cleanup costs for the area and $1 billion in fines and compensatory damages to the state of Alaska. And in September 1994 the firm was ordered by a federal court to pay some $5 billion in punitive damages to the 12,000 to 14,000 plaintiffs in a class action suit by commercial fishermen, Alaskan natives, residents, property owners, and a host of other individuals and groups harmed by the spill. Following the verdict (which will spend years in other courts undergoing the appeal process), each plaintiff stood to gain about $253,000 from the award.

The issue to many of the plaintiffs is not so much the damage done by the oil, but corporate arrogance on Exxon's part. Since the word "punitive" is rooted in the term "punishment," it's no secret that the plaintiffs asked for and got their pound of flesh from Exxon.

As one of the plaintiffs' attorneys put it:

> What our clients really wanted, more than money, is that they're happy with the vindication of seeing Exxon punished. This is the 26th largest economic entity in the world. It's difficult for people like fishermen, cannery workers, and landowners to fight a company like Exxon. It becomes so huge and so arrogant that the company tells the government what to do.[4]

(Of course, anytime someone says, "It's not the money, it's the principle," it's the money.)

For its part, Exxon and its leaders are understandably upset by the award, which must be added to all the other monies they've already spent trying to fix a largely unsolvable problem—the kind that happens when gallons of crude oil and gallons of ocean water mix. Following the verdict (and to his credit as the point man), Exxon Chairman Lee Raymond said the spill was "a tragic accident which impacted the lives of many Alaskans. For that we are truly sorry."[5]

Yet what many people believe to be Exxon's "arrogance" seems to stem from the company's immediate reaction following the action. Being in the supertanker business, it certainly had the required disaster plans in place, even for a spill of this magnitude. Within hours and days, cleanup crews, claims adjusters, maritime accident analysts, and a stream of experts, corporate attorneys, and spokespeople were enroute to the crash site and surrounding area. Once on scene, they got right to work.

And perhaps, in retrospect, that was the problem. These people were so busy doing their jobs that they forgot about the emotional impact of the disaster on the citizens of the area.

In times of great crisis, it may be possible to be *too good* at what you do. The Exxon employees on the scene, going about their business in a highly diligent manner and attempting to offer as much help as they could, first to the company and then to the victims, may have given the impression that this was "just another oil spill" for them.

For the people in the area, however, the spill opened up a floodgate of fears, mostly around the theme of "How is this incident going to affect the rest of our lives and our standard of living?"

By focusing on their tasks and outcomes instead of on the feelings, needs, fears, and apprehensions of the people involved, Exxon as a company may have driven an ever-widening wedge between itself and the people it most needed on its side. And since the people of Alaska already had a love-hate relationship with Big Oil—i.e., love the money, hate the oil rigs and pipelines—the perception that a big company could just come in and throw lots of its money at a problem that was more than just a money issue may have increased the growing resentment.

Is this to say that more brotherly love might have prevented a $5 billion damages award? Knowing human nature and the way attorneys operate in these environments, it's unlikely. But in terms of Exxon's continual harsh beating in the media and as spice for dozens of David Letterman and Jay Leno monologues, perhaps it should have done more to say to its various publics, "We're more than just a huge oil company based in Texas. We have feelings about this incident too. We feel bad that it happened and are just as concerned for your future welfare as we are for ours. We may have different reasons for our worries, but we're willing to listen to you tell us what concerns you most."

This sounds swell in hindsight, of course. But it does address a noticeable gap in Exxon's handling of the incident. Many Alaskan residents who worked and lived in the area did not have the first clue as to what they would do following the spill. They needed help, advice, and a forum in which to vent their feelings and frustrations. Since they couldn't call on Exxon for those things, they turned elsewhere and against the company in all its forms. And then, suddenly, Exxon couldn't do enough, even if it vacuumed up every speck of oil and sent *Valdez* captain James Hazlewood to the North Pole on a drifting iceberg.

As Exxon busied itself with the demands of being a large company, the people who later became plaintiffs seemed to say, "You keep showing us how big and important you are, how many resources you can throw at this problem, and how deep your pockets are. Let's take a closer look at those pockets and see how big and important you really are."

What this incident suggests is that sometimes you have to show people that you care about what's going on in their lives as they interact and intersect with your business—whether they wanted to in the first place or not. Exxon steeled itself to its cleanup and recovery tasks, initiated its full-scale crisis and disaster plans, and yet took its eye off the ball. People don't want to hear about hot-water hose pressure and duck-feather cleaning techniques, they want to see that even a company the size of an Exxon is genuinely sorry, not just that the incident happened, but that it caused lots of problems for lots of people other than itself.

Saying "We're very sorry this happened, both to you and to us" is not an admission of guilt; it's an apology for the fact that a bad thing took place. There is no shame in admitting something your firm did or didn't do caused a mess. To couch this admission in other kinds of languages—i.e., lawyerese, insurance company jargon, or risk-management lingo—is to underestimate the intelligence of your audience.

And besides, is there anyone out there who didn't think Exxon would be sued by every resident, victim, or special interest group attached to the mess?

A genuine and sincere apology from someone in charge can go a long way toward improving the relationship between all the sides involved in a crisis. It's not a sign of weakness; it's a sign of humanity.

Comic Fodder: Image Troubles at the U.S. Postal Service

Pity the poor United States Postal Service; most people do. This organization of over 750,000 employees who go about the business of getting nearly 175 billion pieces of mail into our collective hands every year can get no break from us. The USPS labors under a $47 billion dollar budget (80 percent of which goes for labor costs), which hasn't balanced in decades, and finished 1994 with a deficit approaching $2 billion.

Comedians pepper their monologues with so-called jokes about the Postal Service, hammering on everything from gun-toting wackos gone postal to high stamp prices and ill-mannered clerks. Cartoonists create strips in which postal workers are shown as homicidal, incompetent, or ignorant. Moviemakers have also made the USPS fair game, as the satiric comedy *Naked Gun: 33⅓* demonstrated by opening up with a scene of postal workers armed with machine guns.

To say all this is in the name of plain old fun is wrong. For the people who work at the Postal Service, these depictions are hurtful, mean-spirited, and continue to perpetuate the stereotype that the local post office is both an urban hunting ground waiting to explode and a vacation spot for retired-on-the-job layabouts just waiting for their pension checks.

During a meeting with Postal Service officials in one West Coast city, the director of personnel, the head of HRD, and the director of employee safety each told me the same thing: "All the jokes and comments really hurt our employees' feelings and damage their sense of pride in the work they do and in their organization. Our internal and external image is a big concern for each of us."

Author and Northeastern University professor James Fox points to a number of related items. "It's a combination of factors," he told an Oprah Winfrey audience in 1993. "The post office is typically seen as a high-stress working environment where the employees face constant, never-ending deadlines. And our society doesn't appreciate the work these people do."

Some outsiders believe the job lacks dignity and is usually correctly perceived by most people outside it as blue-collar work. In reality, a Postal Service job is something certain people gravitate toward, probably because of the relatively high pay and the excellent benefits won by the two powerful postal labor unions (the National Association of Letter Carriers and the American Postal Workers) and because the job has a certain civil service steadiness to it. The chances of being fired are still quite slim as long as you do your job adequately, and most people, once settled into the routine of the work, can make a career of it. There are few jobs like it in the government's workforce; it's unique. And there are few private sector jobs that match the pay for the type of work involved.

But back to this idea of image management. Most people still make an easy association between the Postal Service and workplace violence. The sad fact that the themes and concepts surrounding workplace violence have been inextricably linked to the Postal Service really belies the facts. There have been approximately 40 postal worker homicides in the last decade. While that sounds like too many (and even one is tragic), most people don't realize that 15 of those deaths happened in 1986 in Edmond, Oklahoma, when postal employee Patrick Sherrill killed 14 of his co-workers and then himself.

A painful paradox dogs the Postal Service when it comes to the rare workplace shootings that occur on its premises. We have become so accustomed to any form of homicide that what used to be front-page news—i.e., "Worker returns to pickle factory and kills two"—has now been relegated to page 26, bottom of the fold. Many people, in business or otherwise, now take workplace violence for granted. Even homicides in the workplace, which are the smallest but most visible part of the problem, get short attention, except when they happen at a post office.

In April 1993, two postal homicide incidents took place on the same day—one in Dana Point, California, and the other in Royal Oak, Michigan. Within days, we saw bold articles in the *New York Times, USA Today*, and a host of other national magazines and newspapers. All the stories were keyed to one central theme: "What's the problem with these postal people? Why do they keep killing each other?"

The two easiest answers to these questions are: workplace violence inside the Postal Service mirrors workplace violence in the rest of our society, and any organization with three-quarters of a million people (which makes it the nation's largest civilian government employer) is bound to have the same problems as the rest of the adult population and workforce.

The Postal Service is not unique in its employee problems, just more visible. It only took a few shootings before journalists began to think they had uncovered a trend. And then, unfortunately, every incident that followed built upon this supposed legacy of homicide that people think, however incorrectly, plagues the Postal Service only.

There are other issues at the USPS that contribute to its image as an inept organization; most of these have to do with customer service problems that are certainly not unique to any large company in the private sector.

Too often, however, patrons of Postal Service retail service facilities get victimized by some USPS employees whose "I don't care. Here's your stamps. Next!" mentality has given the more hardworking employees a bad name. There is a public perception that these "civil service" workers feel neither civil nor service-oriented.

Further, although we pay some of the lowest rates for stamps in the world, the USPS has failed to manage its image as a money-hogging, money-losing paragovernmental entity that comes around every year with its hand out. In the early 1980s, one postmaster general had the shortsightedness to predict that once first-class stamps reached 25 cents, the rate would hold the USPS for decades. When single-stamp prices rose to 32 cents in January 1995, people looked back on the quarter stamp with nostalgia.

The public tends to blame postal workers for a price increase, as if it were the fault of the clerks at the counter. Though they don't set the price, they must suffer through a series of pointed comments throughout the workday.

Immediate image changes and morale boosters don't seem to be on the horizon for the United States Postal Service. The men and women who work the mail will still take their share of public abuse; top management will still fight for the next rate increase under public criticism and congressional scrutiny; and the media will still run stories like the October 24, 1994, *New Yorker* piece by Jonathan Franzen, "Lost in the Mail," which detailed how thousands of undelivered letters from the Chicago post office were found buried in fields, burned in dumpsters, or stored in letter carriers' homes.

Its sheer size makes changes at the Postal Service much like teaching an elderly elephant to dance. A number of employees have commented that the USPS's poor image is one of the reasons they don't feel proud to say, "I work for the United States Postal Service" without fear of ridicule, hostility, or worse, stupid jokes. Here are a few suggestions that might improve the image and, by proxy, the morale at the USPS. (You can see how some of them might benefit your company's workforce as well.) In terms of enhancing and defending its corporate image and making the employees feel valuable and valued, postal officials might consider:

- *Launching a positive public relations campaign that focuses on Postal Service* people, *not mail handling.* USPS TV and radio ads usually focus on speed of mail service. Most people will agree that they can still get a letter from coast to coast within three or four working days without much trouble. But speedy service is not the issue in terms of its current image; public perception of the organization is what needs rebuilding. As such, why not create an ad campaign that focuses on the human side of the Postal Service? These public service–type messages could show USPS employees as regular folks, with homes and kids, and dogs and cats, and above all, an important job that provides a vital service to the country and the world.

• *Encouraging and rewarding letter carriers who interact with the public on their routes.* There is no sense that we know our mail carrier anymore. He or she walks or drives up to our box, drops the mail inside, and then heads for the next home or business. Why not create a recognition campaign that rewards carriers for taking a bit more time (within reason) to meet and greet the customers on their route? Police departments have started this "get to know us" approach and have found that many people are very receptive to the idea of putting a name to the uniform.

• *De-emphasizing the current paramilitary rank structure now found in senior management.* The USPS operates in a highly structured environment. It follows paramilitary procedures and adheres to titles that don't fit with the public's perception of what it is they do. The leader is called the Postmaster General and his office is filled with Deputy Thises and Chief Thats, just as in the army. And its level of management tends to follow the same paramilitary model, with highly authoritarian, even draconian supervisory procedures in which employees have little margin for error, little leeway for work-related problems, and a constant fear of discipline and sanctions related to demanding and sometimes unachievable job performance and production policies.

• *Offering valid methods for employees to handle the stress of their work.* Management should be as sensitive as possible to the demands that handling the never-ending flow of mail puts on the employees. With automation comes the ability to handle more mail, but more mail still requires people to get it into our boxes.

Courses on anger management, stress control, and employee-to-employee relations should be a part of every worker's ongoing training. The presence of such employee-centered well-being programs can have a positive impact on the public's perception as well, as in, "Look what we're doing for our people."

• *Cleaning house: firing incompetent managers and bad supervisors, toxic or troubled workers, and other people who give the organization a bad name.* This won't happen without major concessions by the postal unions and even outright changes in the civil service laws and procedures. But the fact is that as a large organization, the USPS is filled with some dead wood, just like any other firm of its size and diverse operations. The days of letting bad employees stick around until they retire or go off to be someone else's problem should be over.

Further, why not institute a job rotation policy whereby employees get to change their duties from time to time as a way of keeping themselves fresh? Additionally, the organization could use job reassignments to make sure that the person with the best mail-handling skills but the worst customer service attitude is not stuck behind a retail counter. Frontline service employees should be evaluated for how well they serve the public and rewarded for their efforts with bonuses, time off, or their choice of premium jobs, assignments, or offices.

The Postal Service's current national image needs work. As with any governmental organization, it has some built-in public perception problems at the start. By opening with a premise that says, "We have been in your neighborhood for years and we're here to serve you," the USPS and its people could gradually begin to change the way the public views its work, its workers, and their contribution to society.

In these times, the smallest thing can become a very big deal, literally overnight. Handling these kinds of problems (or, as some might call them, opportunities) calls for a special sensitivity to the people who feel strongly either way about the issues at hand. Companies today are asked to be more socially responsible and keep their inputs, outputs, and practices more in line with the changes in our ever more diverse culture.

When it comes to image problems that require image management, too many companies want to forget the whole nasty event and get back to work. If there are people or groups out to attack your valuable image and the goodwill you've sought to create among your customers, don't let them slip away without demonstrating—through a civil suit, a restraining order, or an injunction—that you're serious about the health and welfare of your company and your employees.

As Procter & Gamble's suits against Amway and Amway's distributors illustrate, your corporate image is worth double its own weight in gold. Just as with a potential product problem, you should vigorously investigate and defend any attack on the image your organization has worked so hard to build.

Notes

1. Levine, Joshua, "Please Excuse Our Shoe Styles of the Past," *Forbes,* January 2, 1995, p. 64.
2. "Snapple Fights Rumor of Racism," *USA Today,* September 2, 1993, p. 2B.
3. Ibid.
4. "Exxon's Penalty $5 Billion in Oil Spill," *San Diego Union-Tribune,* September 17, 1994.
5. Ibid.

5

Employee-Centered and Employee-Related Problems

> The only things that evolve by themselves in an organization are disorder, friction, and malperformance."
>
> —Peter Drucker

To paraphrase cartoon character Pogo, "We have seen the enemy and sometimes he or she works for us." One of the places to look for problems that require corporate self-defense may be right before our eyes.

Among the various scenarios that call for a company and its leaders to spring into a mode of corporate self-defense, many arise from employee problems.

There are event-driven crises that can attack your organization from outside, as we have seen in various cases of product tampering and misuse. And there are situations that can do significant damage to your image and reputation—and again, most of those spring from seeds sown outside the company walls. But there is little doubt that the largest area of liability, the crises that will cause you the most expensive, costly headaches, begin and end with the very people hired and paid to run various parts of the company: your employees.

Let's leave the realms of reason and order for a moment and fantasize into the future. If you took an informal poll of production managers, most would admit that at one point in their careers, they voiced words to this effect: "My employees are driving me crazy! What I wouldn't give for a whole team of robots to take their place!"

Indeed, if we were all able to run our firms using robots, most of our headaches would revolve around maintenance chores such as cleaning and oiling. We wouldn't have to worry about absenteeism caused by home problems—or about sick days, bickering with managers or co-workers, complaints about pay, benefits, or working conditions, or any of the significant and insignificant details that surround people in their working lives.

And frankly, with plenty of well-tuned robots in place, we wouldn't have to worry about the unspeakable acts of business—those actions, episodes, and even crimes that can victimize an organization and its psychological, physical, and financial well-being. There would be no drug or alcohol abuse on the job, no embezzlement, fraud, cheating, or theft. We wouldn't have to worry about employees operating the cash registers without error, driving the forklifts without accident, or walking out with a copy machines under their coats. We wouldn't have to concern ourselves with the ramifications of violence at work, disability claims based upon fake injury claims, or labor-related lawsuits following just-cause terminations.

Now spring back into the real business world, the one where most of these maladies still exist and where, try as we might to create the foundation for a perfectly ethical work environment, things happen.

According to a 1991 report from an Atlanta, Georgia–based employee-polling company known as The Network, the most popular answers to the question "What's hurting your business most?" were employee mistreatment (both by management and other employees) and employee theft.

Nearly 24 percent of 7,200 respondents from 300 different service, retail, and manufacturing firms said that they were concerned about such issues as customer courtesy/service problems, safety violations, equal employment opportunity violations, and substance abuse. Nearly 22 percent of the survey participants reported concerns related to the theft of goods, cash, and time from their firms.

Other significant issues ranged from policy and procedure violations to payroll problems, falsification of company documents, labor law violations, unauthorized discounts, sexual and physical harassment, conflicts of interest, kickbacks, theft or release of proprietary information, defrauding customers, vendor theft, and fraud.[1]

As you will see in Chapter 9, where the discussion of effective corporate self-defense shifts to the need to prevent and defend lawsuits aimed at your firm, most of the problems that force you into a courtroom are related to the conduct and actions of your employees, whether it's the executives, managers, supervisors, or people on the frontline. While we would like to think we have an entire collection of perfectly hard-working, intelligent, and honest employees, the reality today is that one bad apple really can spoil the whole barrel. It's time to look at the way we manage—not just outcomes, but the people we ask to fulfill those goals. We need to look at the way our managers and supervisors hire, coach, empower, lead, counsel, discipline, and terminate their employees as well. And finally, we need to look hard at the way we respond to corporate problems that are directly related to the actions and inactions, deeds and misdeeds, crimes and misdemeanors, and errors in judgment that are caused by the people we bring onboard.

The Blurring Line of Employee-Workplace Problems

An apt metaphor for what goes on at work and what goes on away from work—i.e., at home, or in the streets—is a solid brick wall with WORK printed on one side and HOME on the other. In the past, what we did at home stayed at home, and what we did at work stayed at work.

As late as the latter 1970s and the early part of the 1980s, work problems were work problems and home problems were home problems. And although it was true that certain employees brought their problems back and forth with them, most home problems—like domestic violence, alcohol and substance abuse, and inappropriate sexual behavior—and most psychological maladies—like depression, thoughts of suicide, and other maladjustments due to schizophrenia, kleptomania, and paranoia—were carefully cordoned off from the employer's view.

If employees had these kinds of difficulties in their lives, they tried (with varying degrees of success) to keep them to themselves and away from their co-workers and bosses. The primary reason for this was that employees usually feared for their jobs. "We pay you to work," went the common manager's view, "not to bring your personal problems here. These don't concern us. We're in the business of making products or offering services and otherwise dealing with the needs and concerns of our customers. We're not here to look after you."

This is not to say the above list of employee troubles didn't exist, just that they were more hidden from view, either by the sufferers who kept their troubles quiet or by those who employed them and didn't want to face the consequences of their exposure.

Now, of course, the rules of home and life and work have all changed. Problems with drugs or alcohol, once hushed-up, have now become almost fashionable. Employees are saying to their employers, "I have a drinking or a drug problem. I've tried to deal with it myself, but I can't. Now that *you* know, what are *you* going to do about it? What treatment program will you put me in and pay for?"

As noted in Chapter 2, the employee entitlement syndrome that has affected many organizations has also led to out-of-control problems, such as vandalism, sabotage, rampant theft of goods or data, financially oriented "paper" crimes, domestic violence acted out at the workplace, extortion, intimidation, and other acts and events thought impossible, invisible, or unlikely in the workplace as recently as five years ago.

Some employees have decided that it's now acceptable to act out their frustrations at work. Others have found that since the labor relations deck is clearly stacked in their favor, they can get away with everything short of murder and still keep their jobs. Since the once-solid line between inappropriate behavior at home and inappropriate behavior at work has now gone fuzzy, more people are bringing the worst parts of themselves and their lives to *your* business every day.

Stop Managing Policies and Start Managing People

In defense of the nation's truly effective, honest, and ethical workers, it should be said that some organizations give their employees precious little reward for their hard work and loyalty. In all too many cases, the fault lies not in the way some employees work, but in how their managers treat them.

Some employers are now starting to realize that the function of their business is not just to serve their customers, increase their bottom line, and protect the interests of their shareholders, but also to care for the needs of their most important *internal* customers, their employees.

Gone are the days when you can say, "We make widgets. Our main goal is to make the best widgets possible and serve the customers who buy those widgets. That is our firm's responsibility. Everything else is secondary." While this is good in theory and certainly admirable on paper, it fails miserably as a management operating principle in today's world.

Michael Hammer, co-author of *Reengineering the Corporation,* puts it this way, "The biggest lie ever told by most corporations, and they tell it proudly, is that 'people are our most important assets.' Total fabrication. They treat people like raw material. If you're serious about treating people as an asset, we're looking at a dramatic increase in investment in them."[2]

While Hammer's assessment may sound both obvious and arrogant, it's clear that some company leaders still have not learned their lesson; they continue to mistreat or allow their subordinates to mistreat their employees with unfair, uneven, unethical, or even inhumane policies. These same executives and department heads then have the gall to act surprised when chronic or long-festering employee problems erupt around them.

Whether it comes from a strike that turns from inconvenient to life threatening, as we have seen at firms like the Detroit *Free-Press,* Caterpillar, or Greyhound Bus Lines; or a high-dollar employee theft problem, as happened recently at CompUSA, the computer retailer; or tragic workplace violence incidents that have taken lives at General Dynamics, Ralston, Illinois Bell, Fireman's Fund Insurance, Sumitomo Electric, and Prudential Securities, the quality of worklife is a significant factor in the eyes of most employees in both this and the coming decade.

The issue today is not just how fast, how well, or how often we can make things, answer phones, or rush our products and services out the door. The issue today is how well do we care for the people we hire to do these same things. Do we create a safe, humane working environment with well-enforced rules of conduct and behavior? Are we so strict that the workers feel like prisoners? Or are we so lax that the workers who have questionable ethical values are causing significant problems that affect the bottom line?

Obviously the best answer is to strike a balance between draconian measures designed to keep employees in line and a hands-off "campus" atmosphere, where employees feel as if inappropriate behavior has few if any consequences. The following story illustrates the need to look at the work culture from an environmental standpoint; it's not just tasks and outcomes, it's people and their attitudes and behaviors that make the workplace *work.*

The Bell Captain as Extortionist

As you review this case history, keep the following themes in mind:

- Not all inappropriate employee behavior involves outright theft, destruction, or the willful misuse of company assets.
- Sometimes managers and supervisors can't even see the tip of the iceberg, much less the rest of it.
- Fear among employees can be a powerful motivator and demotivator.

- Negative behavior that shapes the preexisting culture should not drive a manager's decision to make changes. In other words, phrases like "That's just the way things are around here" or "This has gone on for years" are not acceptable answers to inappropriate employee behavior.
- Frontline employees must feel safe and comfortable about communicating with their bosses, or the latter will rarely hear of problems with the former until the damage is done.

Let's meet Bob, a middle-aged bell captain for a large luxury hotel in a major metropolitan city. Bob has been on the job for 15 years, rising from the ranks of bellman to bell captain. Along the way, he has picked up several tricks of the trade, things he learned from senior bell captains as he came up.

Bob now supervises a bell staff of 45, who work in teams of 9, 24 hours per day at the hotel. Since this hotel is near the airport and caters to the business traveler, occupancy is high and the chance to make tips over and above the standard bellman's salary is good. However, much of the extra tip income depends upon location, location, and location. If Bob assigns you to one of his prime spots with lots of activity and much interaction with the guests, you can earn substantial tips. If, on the other hand, you get a post in the hotel's version of eastern Siberia, where few guests need your services, or worse yet, you have to split your tips with the valet parking attendant or the doorman, your income will suffer.

In light of his position and years of experience, Bob knows the best tip spots in the hotel. Under the less-than-watchful eye of the day manager, who has her own work to do and who hasn't been working for the hotel nearly as along as Bob, the location assignments for the bellmen go out on a weekly basis.

Bob's Shake-Down Racket

For his part, Bob learned early on that while his promotion to bell captain led to a raise in pay and stature at the hotel, it also served to drastically reduce his own tip income. To combat this economic loss, Bob has developed a system—or more correctly, he inherited it from his predecessors.

Bob now shakes down the bellmen stationed at the best locations in the hotel. After they have worked for him for a short time, he suggests to them politely that if they want a spot where they will be guaranteed good tips, they will have to pay him a cash "gift" each week before he prepares the schedule.

Those who refuse—and they are few in number—get both the worst assignments and heavy-handed treatment from Bob. On a few occasions, he has threatened, shoved, and even punched staff members he feels have been "uncooperative" about paying.

In addition to such use of force and the exiling of uncooperative bellmen to empty meeting rooms, the kitchen, or ceremonial stations where no guests ever need help, Bob makes offhand comments to other managers that these people are not "team players."

Bob's system also includes other low-paid hotel staffers who struggle for tips. He gets a cut from the valet parking attendants, the door staff, and even some of the room service waiters. They pay him because he is the senior hourly employee at the hotel and it is in his power to make their burdens at work lighter or heavier.

Somewhere along the line, the phrase "the best way to get along is to go along" becomes a part of the work culture, and the workers with strong personalities have convinced the others not to make waves. So Bob's little fear-based operation—modeled after the protection racket idea used by members of organized crime—flourishes week after week when the schedules come out and the employee billfolds open up. Bob's boss is too harried in her job to check into his staffing procedures. As far as she knows, her guests are getting their baggage needs met and she hears no complaints from the hotel staff. It's just business as usual.

What to Do With an Employee Like Bob

The moral of this (unfortunate but true) story is summed up in a series of questions: What is the impact upon the organization? In other words, what does Bob's employee-centered extortion-ring-in-miniature do to the rest of the hotel? What impact does his coercion have upon his subordinates and the other people who encounter him with his hand out? Even if you could argue that the dollar figures are small and the problem is confined to the hourly staff, isn't this a serious employee-created and employee-centered problem? Isn't there a potential for further threats and violence, future workplace criminal acts by Bob or his cohorts, and/or a civil suit for allowing a "hostile working environment" to flourish?

This is where Bob's supervisor should start to earn her manager's pay. She must investigate and recognize Bob's behavior as aberrant, harmful to the hotel and its workers, expensive in a variety of forms, illegal in many aspects, and just plain wrong. In other words, it's time to step in, interview every employee (without the threat of job loss or informal sanctions by others for ratting on Bob), gather all the information—dates, times, places, amounts—make copies of the schedules and review them, and then speak to the head of the hotel's human resources department about this problem.

Armed with the hard data, the interviews, and the backing of the HR office, it's then time to bring Bob in, confront him with the facts of his long-running misdeeds, and unceremoniously fire him.

The problem in dealing with Bob and employees of his ilk is that, while many supervisors would agree that this kind of behavior borders on the illegal, is tremendously disruptive, and is worthy of an immediate management intervention, their fallback position is, "We know it's not right, but what can we do about it?"

Confronting inappropriate employee behavior is not fun. Most of us dislike conflict and confrontation—so much so that we would rather turn a blind eye to what we know in our hearts is wrong, just to avoid having to confront an employee and say, "What you're doing is clearly in violation of our policies. Your last day is today." If this inability or unwillingness to sit an employee down and have the hard talk describes you or managers in your firm, a change is called for.

In many respect, Bob is a corporate terrorist. His oppressive and even violent behavior intimidates the other employees to such a degree that they cannot function at normal productivity levels. (How hard or well would *you* work if you had the threat of another weekly shakedown or a punchout hanging over your head?)

One of the best ways to help managers deal with this kind of inside agitation is to get help. No one says you have to deal with these kinds of out-of-the ordinary problems alone. Tell your managers to ask for assistance from any department or department heads who can help them achieve this difficult but necessary outcome—getting rid of that small percentage of the employee population that engages in unethical, illegal, violent, or clearly inappropriate behavior.

This could include the creation of a company discipline or termination team made up of various department heads or managers who have experience in the areas of both employer and employee rights in these issues. After reviewing each case on an as-needed basis, they can help the manager or supervisor initiate safe, careful, and legal discipline or termination procedures.

There *is* safety in numbers. Supervisors who fail to act in these cases usually say that they fear the legal ramifications and they don't how to initiate the process. Give them the resources they need to feel empowered. The company they save from employees like Bob the Extortionist belongs to everyone, and his loss is their gain.

Facing the Fear of Death on the Job

While Bob's story illustrates the presence of low-level violence in the workplace, the stakes have been raised much higher in most of the more well-publicized cases. Incidents of pushing and shoving in the employee break room have been superceded by sounds of gunfire.

Indeed, a whole new vocabulary has grown up around the expanding concept of violence in the workplace, including such phrases as "going postal" to suggest aggressive or violent behavior; "ticking bombs" to describe potentially disturbed or violence-prone individuals; and the oft-used "disgruntled ex-employee" who returns to the workplace after a suspension or a termination wielding a gun.

What used to be a front-page news story is now relegated to page 26, especially as we get more and more desensitized to acts of workplace violence, even homicide. While murder on the job is rare, it has risen to become the number-two cause of death for men at work and, more disturbingly, the number-one cause of death for women on the job.

Like incidents of sexual harassment, workplace violence can cost a company significant amounts of money, paid out under disability claims, stress retirements, and civil suits for allowing problems to go unheeded or uncorrected.

The United States Postal Service estimates that the 1986 incident involving Edmond, Oklahoma, postal worker Patrick Sherill, who took 14 lives and then his own, has cost the organization $25 million. Take that figure right to the bottom line of their profit-and-loss sheets every time you buy a stamp.

An increasingly disturbing relative of workplace violence is domestic violence in the workplace, where the suspect may not have any connection to the organization save for his partner.

A recent case near Omaha, Nebraska, illustrates this trend. A distraught man, estranged from his common-law wife, waited outside the computer assembly plant where she worked and shot her and her new boyfriend to death, before (as often happens) turning the gun on himself. This was the second similar incident in six years at that factory. The trend is not the fault of the factory operators; it simply points out the way some disturbed people solve their problems today.

The Omaha case is a timely example, but it's far from the only one. A rental car agency in Dallas was the scene of a shooting when a terminated employee returned with a gun and shot and wounded his ex-girlfriend and her boss. Another incident in Santa Fe Springs, California, involved an electronics worker who shot and killed several colleagues after a female co-worker spurned his romantic advances.

What message does a workplace homicide or other significant domestic violence event send to other women in the organization who have their own hidden relationship-abuse problems? And what message does it send to all the employees, especially if top management knew about it and yet failed to take appropriate action?

In the past, these kinds of problems might have been handled with no police involvement whatsoever. Companies and their leaders often took a position that amounted to "We'll handle this in-house," which is another way of saying, "God forbid that our customers, vendors, stockholders, competitors, or the media should find out about this."

This point of view is changing, thanks both to increased media attention and to the real possibility that companies can be sued for failing to intervene with all available resources. In other words, if they knew about the problem and failed to offer a range of solutions, they can be held liable.

In terms of corporate self-defense, it's time to see the specter of violence in the workplace and domestic violence arriving or ending in the workplace as part of our new business realities. Handling these problems calls for a united effort by top management, the human resources department, security managers in the organization, and even local law enforcement.

As more and more people choose violence as a way to strike back at either the company or its people, it is up to the firm's leaders and managers to initiate as many safety and protection plans as possible.

Labor Disputes: No Longer One Big Happy Family

Organized labor finds itself at an eerie crossroads here in the 1990s. With union membership down, and many companies turning to closed-shop relationships, Big Labor's most powerful weapon has been blunted; the threat of a general strike or other organized labor stoppage device no longer carries the same clout.

Today, companies faced with the realities of a long strike

make no secret of the fact that, should one occur, they will take immediate steps to hire replacement workers. Whereas labor unions used to be able to threaten the viability of the company by shutting down most of its key operations, the desire by many underemployed or unemployed people to cross a picket line is strong enough to remove much of the teeth from the threat.

In effect, labor unions are having their bluffs called by management teams who say, "Strike if you must, but we will get injunctions to prevent you from blocking our gates. We will ask your members to return to work voluntarily, and if they don't, we'll hire replacement workers and bus them into the facilities every day. We'll use our own guard service or contract with a security firm to protect our people and property from your harm. And we will wait and see who has more staying power."

This is not to say that a strike cannot be a powerful weapon when aimed at certain industries, but the days of Samuel Gompers are long gone. Plenty of people on the outside see strikes as an opportunity for them to get a better, higher-paying job by crossing the picket lines. And many people walking the picket lines see no victory in marching for no strike pay, no benefits, and the distinct possibility of replacement even if the strike ends.

As the strike that began at the Detroit *Free-Press* newspaper plant in August 1995 illustrated, it's hard for both sides to think of themselves as part of a team when the strikers are throwing rocks and bottles at the police and the members of management can't get through the front doors thanks to the picketers, sign-swingers, and tear gas.

The Detroit *Free-Press* management failed to take the proper prestrike legal steps: They did not get an immediate injunction against the strikers and therefore were forced to use the police and security guards to move them from blocking the access gates. They also failed to have strike contingency plans in effect: they hadn't worked out how to get blank newsprint into the plant and printed papers back out again. Finally, plant management failed to manage the company's image with the national media; photos of clashing police and picketers filled the front pages of other papers, only serving to intensify the newspaper's problem in the minds of the various publics who viewed the conflict.

Your best weapon in any strike-related event lies with the members of two departments: labor relations and security. They should have contingency plans on file for any labor-related problems.

As a corporate self-defense issue, labor problems offer a combination of management anxieties, security concerns, the threat of violence, customer or shareholder confidence problems, and the real but rarely discussed issue of what happens when the strike, stoppage, or slowdown ends and everyone goes back to work. How will management and labor get along, especially in light of the conflicts raised during these events? Who will mediate the subsequent personality clashes as each side tries to get back to work?"

Internal Shrinkage: A Rose by Any Other Name

H. L. Mencken once said, "An idealist is one who, on noticing that a rose smells better than a cabbage, concludes that it will also make better soup."

Calling theft by employees by the popular and vaguely oxymoronic euphemism "internal shrinkage," is like referring to murder as a "death accident." It's hard to determine where or when the phrase "internal shrinkage" originally reached our business vocabulary, but its use should be outlawed as a vain attempt to put a sugarcoated handle on a serious organizational problem—the theft of your products, services, and other assets by your employees. In effect, Mencken was right; you can't make something taste good by giving it a pretty name, especially when it's a billion-dollar problem.

As we speak of this rank idealism, consider that *twice* as much is stolen from companies by *employees* than by outsiders. I'll repeat this for emphasis: More of your products and inventory leave illegally by the employee exit than by the customer exit.

So why is it that retail establishments spend so much of their time and money hiring uniformed store guards and undercover security and attaching sensors to their merchandise, all in an effort to catch people who come into their stores, when the shoplifters who most victimize them are already on the payroll?

This is not to say that every employee steals or that all employees are dishonest. But as much as we'd like to believe that it's a ring of professional thieves who swipe our merchandise, or a group of cat burglars who scale the roofs and come in after hours, or teenagers who pocket our CD's, cosmetics, and sporting goods, they are a small part of the theft problem.

W. Roger Curry, the CEO of package shipper Emery Worldwide, refers to this type of theft or fraud committed against a business, especially by its own employees, as "business abuse."[3] And he's right; this kind of behavior is being committed by the very people we expect to help protect our assets. So let's stop calling it "internal shrinkage" and start referring to it by its real name: *the theft of merchandise and assets by employees.*

And if you're in search of even more irony, consider the galling fact that many managers justify their knowledge of employee theft with a generic reply, "It's just a cost of doing business. What can we do about it? Search everyone before they leave at the end of the day?"

Speaking to a reporter about theft by customers and employees, one store manager as much as admitted to throwing in the towel: "If you get paranoid about security, you're only going to scare off good customers. I just pray that I don't get ripped off too much."[4]

In their book *Are Your Employees Stealing You Blind?* authors Edwin C. Bliss and Isamu S. Aoki estimate that fully 75 percent of workers steal from their employers at least once.[5] How much more do you need to know?

It's time to confront this problem at the managerial level, admit that it exists, and then set about protecting the company from further harm by putting the right security measures and theft countermeasures in place. Ultimately, you *do* have a duty and responsibility to your employees (the honest ones who don't steal from you), your customers (to see that their goods arrive untouched by thieves, that they and their property are safe inside your facility, and that they won't have to pay inflated prices for your goods to justify your expenses related to employee theft), and to your shareholders to keep costs down.

It's amazing that some company managers and even some company owners can justify employee theft as "one of those things we'd like to control but just haven't got around to." If you were to suggest to them that a burglar will come into their house every day while they are gone and steal one or two of their personal belongings, would their attitude about theft change? Absolutely! You would see a new sense of energy about this problem; they would install protection devices, increase their awareness of who comes and goes, and make it as hard as humanly possible for the thief to get into their homes.

The message your organization needs to ring from its bell towers is this:

> *Security is everybody's business. The protection of our people and property starts with your awareness of potential problems, your ability to observe and report security issues to the proper departments, and your willingness to be alert. This company belongs to everyone, and the employee who steals from one of us steals from all of us.*

Preventing employee theft boils down to one theme: attitude. If top management gives the problem short shrift, if middle management turns its collective head away, the opportunistic employees who do steal from their company will continue to ply their art. Marginal employees who steal from the organization need only to see tacit approval of their actions. If the bosses condone this behavior as "just one of those things" and there is no sense of the ramifications, punishment if they're caught, or other hard-and-fast intervention by management, the problem will continue and flourish.

Do you want your firm to develop a reputation as an easy target? Do you want unethical employees (and their outside cohorts) to see your company as one big fat golden goose, ready for plucking? Do you see your products, equipment, inventory, and assets as valuable? If so, it's time to eradicate the phrase "internal shrinkage" from your vocabulary and replace it with "We will do whatever it takes to protect this company from theft, no matter who does it."

If You Want to Steal, Don't Use a Gun, Get a Keyboard

As if you didn't have enough to protect your company from, computer technology has created an entire new industry of crime. Whether it comes from hacking into systems for the purpose of wandering around a company's files, sheer vandalism (inserting viruses, erasing files, sabotaging existing files, etc.), or the unauthorized and illegal transfer of money, data, or trade secrets, computer crime is a reality.

As G. Green and R. J. Fischer put it in their corporate security book, "Probably no one element in business presents a greater potential to wipe out an entire business as quickly and so effectively as the computer."[6]

Yet many firms don't report these rip-offs, illegal entries, or damage to law enforcement, largely because they don't know whom to call. Do they contact their local police, sheriff's office, the FBI, the Secret Service? The answer to all these is yes; call each of these groups, starting with the police and then working your way up to the federal agencies, depending upon the dollar amounts lost, the type of crime, the data and value of the information stolen or manipulated. Report these incidents and let the professionals help you make the right prosecution or enforcement decisions.

Still other firms believe that the turmoil surrounding these events—the aftereffects and changes that must be made—outweighs the decision to contact authorities. In short, they believe it's cheaper to chalk the incident up to experience than to absorb the costs from such things as security or data audits; policy and procedure changes; employee transfers, discipline, or terminations; legal fees, civil suits, or the damage to their reputation in the business community if their victimization were exposed.

Rip-offs involving computers occur when: opportunistic employees load other workers' computers into the backseats of their cars and never return them; manipulative employees steal their own laptops and then report them as stolen; or highly specialized burglars, like those striking in the Silicon Valley, take machines, parts, and those expensive (but easily stolen, stored, and resold) computer chips.

And there are also growing threats to your company's information security. We already know that the incidence of internal theft is twice as high as external theft, so it should come as no surprise that the people who take your proprietary data include current, disgruntled, or past employees; internal subcontractors, consultants, or vendors; competitors; and other individuals or groups who see what you have on paper or online as valuable.

Much of the fault for this theft of information lies in poorly written and poorly enforced policies and procedures regarding data protection. If the employee culture doesn't seem to care about or impose sanctions for repeated breaches of information security, we can see the same vicious circle appear as with other employee thefts: "The more they don't care, the more I can get away with."

With all the high-tech rip-off possibilities around today, your E-mail, voice mail, and telephone systems, and your fax, cellular phone, and modem lines are no longer impenetrable. If you think this kind of hacking and illegal access only happens in the movies, consider the fact that a small Texas oil pipe firm lost out on a major contract when a competitor hacked into its private voice-mail lines. After the two men assigned to win the contract had left each other messages about their bids and pricing information, their competitors successfully broke into their voice-mail system, extracted the valuable information without their knowledge, and proceeded to underbid the contract enough to win it.

The only saving grace from this story comes in the form of retribution. After an investigation, the participants in this new brand of corporate espionage were caught and indicted. The small firm was awarded the contract.

As with ways of preventing employee theft, you can make a dent in information or technology theft. This might include: getting a commitment from top management to attack the problem; hiring information security experts and having them audit your data security procedures for flaws; asking your security staff to train managers and employees in data security precautions and procedures; and then asking these informed employees to practice voluntary security compliance.

Sexual Harassment: The More Things Change, the More They Stay the Same

While there is little or nothing positive you can say about on-the-job sexual harassment (save for the fact that its perpetrators often get theirs in the end), the spate of high-profile cases (the Navy Tailhook saga and the $1.2 million Del Labs case in New York, for instance) has served an effective purpose by raising the overall awareness level of this workplace abuse.

In that respect, many companies and their personnel specialists who in the past turned a deaf ear to such claims, cases, incidents, and allegations, have now tackled sexual harassment prevention steps in earnest. And while we'd like to think that their reasons are based on their outrage against past abuses, their solid ethical stance, or their respect for the rights of both female and male victims, the real reason is largely based on cash.

Sexual harassment lawsuits can be outrageously expensive for the defendant company and its alleged perpetrators. While few of these cases ever reach the jury trial stage—usually due to settlements prior to court hearings or following preliminary hearings, or to other arbitration sessions—the ones that do go through the jury trial can cost defendant organizations hundreds of thousands, even millions of dollars. In other words, you will comply with newer, stricter guidelines concerning sexual harassment prevention, or you will pay for it later.

A San Francisco Superior Court jury agreed with plaintiff Rena Weeks that her boss, Baker & McKenzie attorney Martin Greenstein, had sexually harassed her for the three-plus weeks she worked for him. The court awarded her $225,000 to be paid by Greenstein and a record-setting $6.9 million to be paid by the firm. In the jury's opinions, Baker & McKenzie, the world's largest law firm, with 1,700 lawyers and $70 million in net income, had failed to monitor or correct the situation once it became apparent. Supporters of the verdict said in press accounts that it sent the right message, not only to future harassers, but to their employers as well.

There is still a segment of the adult and largely male working population who will not buy in to any form of sexual harassment awareness or prevention training, no matter how it is offered to them. Instead of complaining to all who will listen that despite your efforts, you just can't make your company a "zero-tolerance, harassment-free" workplace, do your best, exhibit due diligence, deal with your successes, and fight hard to avoid defeats.

In other words, if you provide the training, offer investigation activities, employee support and guidance, and clamp down hard on potential or ongoing instigators, you have done nearly all you can do.

While the halls of justice are filled with stories and cases of companies who lost thousands of dollars due to lax prevention policies, poor or nonexistent training, failures to intervene, and lousy supervision practices, there are firms that did all the right things and later persevered in court.

The popular restaurant chain TGI Friday's found itself in a San Diego, California, court facing charges of sexual harassment from six female employees. The women charged that between 1990 and 1992, the restaurant allowed "a hostile work environment" to grow—so much so that they were forced to quit their jobs.

If you've ever eaten at a TGI Friday's restaurant, you know it's a place known for its fun atmosphere, extensive menu, and for many employees who enjoy dressing up their work uniforms with wild hats, catchy buttons and slogans, and other paraphernalia to show that Friday's is a hip place to eat and work.

The women claimed that the Friday's general manager and his assistant manager engaged in sexually harassing behavior, including gestures, remarks, and inappropriate touching.

Here's the interesting part: while the court ordered the general manger to pay *punitive* damages to one of the women, it held that the Friday's restaurant and the chain itself was *not* liable for the actions of its two male employees.

Surprised? Here's the reason TGI Friday's prevailed in court:

- It offered sexual harassment training to all new employees.
- It offered ongoing sexual harassment training to all employees.
- Prior to these claims, the company had maintained a twenty-four-hour hotline and encouraged its employees to use it to report work-related complaints.

In overturning the women's claims, the court said that while the male employees engaged in inappropriate behavior, the female employees did not help the restaurant initiate an investigation because they had failed to report the behavior until after they had quit the company.

The Friday's victory with regard to sexual harassment litigation suggests the need for you to establish two important criteria in your own organization:

1. Have a strong policy against it, which starts with new employee training, no-tolerance policies, ongoing, in-service training, and a bona fide complaint-gathering system.
2. Follow up on any complaints or charges immediately, including immediate, thorough, and confidential interviews with witnesses, victims, and subject employees, and appropriate counseling, discipline, or termination for the instigators.

A Table for Our Attorney: Denny's and Diversity

The management of people and their duties is difficult under any circumstances, but it can be doubly hard if the parent company is in one place and the employees are in another. Their problems can become your problems in a terrible hurry.

Denny's, the coffee shop restaurant chain, found itself embroiled in a huge public controversy related to race discrimination. In March 1993, the U.S. Justice Department claimed that Denny's restaurants in California had denied service to black customers and forced other blacks to pay for their meals in advance. This led later to the forced creation of an in-house Denny's watchdog/race relations committee that now offers sensitivity training for the company.

The root of this problem was—as is the theme in this chapter—an employee-centered one. The individual restaurant managers either engaged in this discriminatory behavior or allowed their employees to do it. And if even if they didn't practice this invasive form of customer selection, they were still to blame for allowing it to occur while on their watch.

This collection of incidents reinforces the need for the parent company to keep a weather eye on its individual outlets. "Out of sight, out of mind" should not be the catch-phrase that allows this kind of racially demeaning behavior to continue. It's initially up to the parent company to set the tone, i.e.:

> This is how we will treat all our customers regardless of their outward appearance. This is how we expect you to treat your customers when they come into well over one thousand of our Denny's restaurants. We will ask our national, regional, and district managers to follow these same procedures and to see that you and your employees are doing the same.

It appears from these incidents that the Denny's parent company fell into a trap common to companies with many locations: one hand doesn't know what the other is doing. In its efforts to run the day-to-day operations at the corporate level, make the big decisions, and set the direction of the company, Denny's management forgot one important point:

> What goes on at the frontline, grassroots, customer level is what affects your business the most. Unhappy customers don't come back, and worse yet, if they tell their families, friends, co-workers, and in this case, the national media, about their level of treatment at one of your restaurants, it could start to look as though your organization is out of control.

Denny's other failing in this incident was its handling of the media. It made little sense to argue the point in print, especially when one of the victims was a group of six black U.S. Secret Service officers. And more shockingly, during the six years before the uproar, the company had garnered some 4,000 customer complaints of racial bias. In May 1994, the firm settled a $46 million class-action suit filed on behalf of hundreds of angry black patrons in conjunction with the U.S. Justice Department. There is a time to fight for your rights as an organization and a time to admit you made an error that demands correction.

At least Jerome Richardson, the head of Denny's holding company, Flagstar Co., had the sense to make several public appearances to discuss the problem with black civil rights leaders. To ignore their concerns, especially in light of what was clearly inappropriate behavior on the part of several Denny's chains and employees, would have only made a galling situation worse.

This image problem for Denny's illustrates the power of the media as a watchdog for illegal, unethical, or discriminatory practices. Had Denny's executives been more cognizant of their frontline supervisors and employees, this problem might not have turned into a $46 million public relations nightmare.

The Decline of the Ethical Work Environment

Companies and their leaders have the right to run their organizations as they see fit, just as employees have the right to work there or not. It's time to discuss the best ways to bring these two often-disparate groups together on the same ethical page. Since tough times call for tough measures, let's look at something known as the *Ethical Contract.*

Consider your firm's need to create an official, legally enforceable document that every current and new employee must read, sign, and be able to explain. In it, your company will outline what is and what is not appropriate work behavior, based on some agreed-upon descriptions.

The actual wording of this contract between the company and the employee may vary greatly, depending upon the nature of the work, the established culture, the need for extra security (as with Department of Defense–related contracts), and the degree to which you want to create a form that tries to account for every legal or behavioral possibility.

Some firms create a document of this nature in order to explain zero-tolerance policies for such things as employee drug abuse, drinking on the job, violence, the use or possession of weapons at work, inappropriate or abusive language, physical or sexual harassment, theft, vandalism, gambling, and racial bias. On paper and in clear language, this document should tell all who read and discuss it:

> *We are deeply committed to protecting this company, its people, its interests, its reputation, its assets, its customers, and its relationship with the community.*
>
> *It is now time for honesty in all that we do, how we treat each other, how we expect to be treated, and how we expect all employees to respect the property, privacy, and lifestyles of everyone who comes here.*
>
> *It is now time to get back to a more law-and-order version of business life. As such, we will not tolerate any of the following activities, behaviors, or crimes.* (Use the above list as a starting point.)
>
> *It is now time for managers to stop coddling employees with significant behavioral problems. We will offer counseling and progressive discipline, but failing that, you can*

expect to be terminated if you engage in the unethical, illegal, or inappropriate behaviors listed above.

We plan to increase our rewards for honest, ethical employees and increase the punishments for dishonest, unethical employees.

We will set up enforcement activities, deterrent activities, greater security controls, and other protection steps for the benefit of the innocent and for the prosecution of the guilty.

We will insist that our executives, managers, and supervisors exhibit the highest ethical qualities at all times and model those behaviors for their employees. We would hope that this sense of the need for ethical behavior while at work will become part of every employee's approach to his or her job and working relationships with others.

We will strive to create an ethical, fair, and humane culture here. We will provide specific training in the areas of ethics, security, and leadership, for both our management and frontline staff.

We encourage all employees to discuss their concerns and offer feedback about the problems or opportunities they see as we all strive to create an ethical environment.

We will expect all employees to understand our position as it pertains to appropriate work behavior. All employees will be asked to review, discuss, and sign a document stating that they understand what is expected of them and what, in turn, they can expect from the organization.

Some written form of the above can get you on the right road toward creating a workplace environment that is free of many of the employee-created crises that now plague other companies. With today's questionable morals and the standards set by the entitled or disgruntled employee, it falls to the organization and its leaders to keep problem employees and their unwanted activities from piercing the corporate walls.

Notes

1. "What's Hurting Business Most? Employee Mistreatment, Theft," *San Diego Business Journal,* October 12, 1993, p. 5.
2. "Training Today," *Training Magazine,* April 1995, p. 20.
3. "Jargon Quiz," *Training Magazine,* September 1994, p. 84.
4. Green, Frank, "Grand Larceny," *San Diego Union-Tribune,* December 18, 1994, p. I-3.
5. Bliss, Edwin C., and Isamu S. Aoki, *Are Your Employees Stealing You Blind?* (San Diego, Calif.: Pfeiffer, 1994).
6. Green, G., and R. J. Fischer, *Introduction to Security* (Boston: Butterworth, 1987), p. 326.

Part Two

Self-Defense Tools for Your Organization

6

Arming the Company SWAT Team

The First Responders

> It often happens that I wake at night and begin to think about a serious problem and decide I must tell the Pope about it. Then I wake up completely and remember that I am the Pope.
>
> —Pope John XXIII

Most company policies and procedures are designed to handle routines, not uncommon events. Part of the reason for a firm's inability to deal with a pending or sudden crisis is that no one or no group in the organization has been given the real position of designated responder. This chapter speaks to your need to create, staff, or equip a crisis response/crisis management team.

No matter what the size of the company, someone in top management must take the responsibility for action, leadership, and direction during any out-of-the-ordinary event. This person doesn't have to be the CEO or company owner, but the decision and the subsequent order to create this position must come from that level.

Just as the Federal Aviation Administration has a response team of accident investigators who race at a moment's notice to the scene of every airline crash, so should every organization have its own response team. Whether the group is made up of 5 people or 25, those involved must, along with their other regular workday duties, be ready to step in and institute an already-created plan of action for any serious problem that turns the organization on its ear.

It's time to discuss how to create and staff your response team, how to formulate plans for a variety of events, how to commit those plans to paper, and more importantly, how to get the executives, managers, frontline supervisors, and the employees to buy into the various plans, roles, and responsibilities and help to activate them.

> Any company that is totally surprised by a serious product, service, image, or employee problem is badly managed.

As the old plumber says, "The time to look for the water supply cutoff valve is *before* the pipes have broken, not after." The time to write your plans, indoctrinate your response personnel, and otherwise commit your firm's energy and resources to this kind of problem solving is now, not when the water reaches your eyebrows.

Any effective response starts with avoiding the problem in the first place. Risk management surveys, risk assessments, and other proven methods for recognizing and then minimizing catastrophes should already be a given in your organization. Whether these fact-finding missions are conducted by members of your risk department, security office, safety coordinator, attorney, insurance agent, or other problem-locating expert, it makes sense for senior management to know what needs fixing before it breaks. With a risk assessment on paper, you can focus on what needs your immediate attention, organize your tasks in order of severity, importance, and time deadlines, then take action should one of the noted items become a reality.

If you don't have a good definition for the phrase "due diligence" in your organization, talk to your in-house legal department or outside corporate attorney and get one. In its briefest descriptions, due diligence refers to just that:

[Have you and your firm been duly diligent in your efforts to recognize potential problems and/or crises and then offer either plans to prevent them or solutions if they appear?]

As an example, the phrase *hostile working environment* is one lawsuit-related term frequently attached to employee claims of sexual harassment, racial problems, workplace violence, or unlawful discipline or termination procedures. If the plaintiffs can prove that your managers knew of existing or growing problems in these areas, and yet did nothing to intervene, take corrective actions, or otherwise attempt to solve the problem in a timely and legal manner, it may be possible for the plaintiffs to prove that your firm did not exhibit the necessary due diligence in the handling of these issues.

Should your situation end up in civil court, judges, attorneys, and juries will want to know if you did your best to head off problems before they began and what steps you took at the onset of any serious event to demonstrate that you knew whom to call (inside or outside your organization), when to call them, and what to have them do for you.

Staffing the Crisis Response Team

Most managers working within their organizations are no strangers to committees. Organizing your firm's crisis response/crisis management team may not be seen as either mandatory or fun by those who don't understand its function or their role in what looks like a dreary assignment. And since you can't make cod liver oil taste any better by calling it honey, it's best to draft your participants quickly, set a meeting date and time that is close to this first call, and get to the business at hand.

You'll want to draw from among the company's sharpest people, and this includes all related department heads, key executives, and managers. Be selective, but keep company protocol and the nature of the project and the organizational hierarchy in mind.

In a perfect world, in which you had access to all the best minds money could buy, unlimited assets, and piles of cash at your disposal, you could create a team that would rival something found in the pages of a Tom Clancy novel. But back in the real world, with limited personnel, dwindling assets, and budget restrictions, you have to make do with the most your firm can offer. We will look at several different staffing suggestions, based on the size of your company, the number and type of its departments, and the understanding that some team members may have to perform more than one function in a real crisis situation. We'll look at each position and the duties required in some detail.

If you've got the clout of a midsize or large firm behind you, consider this number and type of crisis-response team members:

Chief Executive Officer

For this kind of committee/crisis response team concept to function effectively (not perfectly, but close), there must be a Chief in charge of the Indians. Someone must take on the role of ultimate leader and final decision maker, be it the CEO or another similar ranking chief officer. This helps keep department-head ego battles out of the group's operations and it unifies the team under a recognizable chain of command.

It also helps to establish a link between the senior executives, who may have one set of agendas, and the middle managers, who may have another. Someone has to give the orders to the people who give the orders. While it's not necessary to set up a military model, the highest-ranking executive should serve as the figurehead for your operations.

Director of Human Resources Development

In many organizations, the person in charge of Human Resource Development (HRD) serves as the overseer of most employee-related functions. As such, he or she should already have a finger on the pulse of the people side of the house. The HRD officer may also have intimate knowledge of the labor relations issues facing the company, the existing quality of worklife issues, and a feeling of the general climate and culture in the organization as it relates to the employees, the supervisors, and top management.

During the span of a serious event, it will be up to this person to manage and protect the human assets of the company as well as possible.

Director of Personnel

The director of personnel serves as the gatekeeper to the company's personnel practices, policies, and records. In any serious event, the integrity of all these elements must be protected.

Like the head of HRD, the Director of Personnel also should be well aware of the issues and events that concern the employees. In a crisis, this person can help with staffing requirements, manpower allocations, legality questions, union negotiations, and questions or steps relating to discipline and termination procedures.

Director of Training

A few caveats need to be discussed prior to the training director's inclusion in the crisis response team. In some firms, this position is included as part of the overall HRD function. In other firms, the training function is not taken seriously, and therefore, by extension, neither is the person who runs this department. If the person in charge here is not strong enough to make the executives see training as a corporate necessity, his or her ideas may not be given much consideration by top management.

In those firms where the training director *is* an integral part of management, he or she can give valuable information in a crisis, especially as it relates to past training in issues that may now face the company: hazardous-materials classes; first aid, CPR, and fire training; quality control, inspection, and production training; personnel, supervision, and management training; and any other programs that may be called upon in a court of law or the court of public opinion to demonstrate that the company is current, legal, and up to date in its procedures.

Director of Information Services

If the firm is large enough to have an Information Services (IS) department, its director will need to provide significant input into the data and information protection strategies. We see plenty of media accounts of the rampant theft of company data by insiders and outsiders, the theft or misuse of proprietary software, espionage, and hacking into files and accounts by everyone from teenagers to agents from foreign governments.

With the prevalence of the Internet, the World Wide Web, and the growing number of on-line services, we will see more of this kind of criminal behavior, in which the thief or vandal uses a keyboard instead of a gun.

Increasingly, the IS officer will be called upon to protect the company from threats from both without and within.

Director of Security

As I will discuss with security expert Gavin de Becker in Chapter 10, the director of security *must* have access to senior management on a continual basis. To be most effective, the security director should provide input into decisions related to personnel problems—hiring, discipline, and termination procedures.

He or she also should know (or have employees who know) how to provide high-tech security procedures to protect the company's data, information secrets, computers, and electronic components (standard and cellular phones, fax machines, modem lines, etc.). It is critical, especially in high-risk situations, that these devices work *for* the company and not against it.

As recent highly publicized experiences demonstrate, the person in charge of the security department has to wear a number of different name tags, from manager to investigator, from security officer to trainer. In any potentially dangerous, violent, or disaster-prone event, this person will bear most of the weight when it comes to protecting the company's physical, psychological, and human assets.

Director of Employee Assistance Programs

Like the security director, the director of Employee Assistance Programs (EAP) usually spends most of his or her time trying to solve employees' personal problems. Whether they're related to medical, psychological, or financial difficulties, the head of EAP regularly sees a cornucopia of crisis-related events, if not for the firm, then for the employees embroiled in them.

What makes this person valuable as a crisis response team member is his or her built-in access to so many different outside resources who can help the firm. Many EAP directors have an entire Rolodex devoted to "outside" phone numbers for counselors, social service providers, therapists and psychologists, labor law experts, legal help, medical doctors, medical specialists, and related experts, and any other function that relates to the well-being of the workforce.

Legal Affairs/Corporate Counsel

In many cases, your firm's in-house attorney may be one of the first to hear or see a crisis situation in the making. He or she will likely be the agent of service for any civil papers and the usual recipient of any letters from other attorneys, people, or groups that threaten legal action against the organization.

If this person has any experience at all as a courtroom litigator, he or she may be one of the coolest heads on the crisis response team. With lawsuits on the minds of everyone—both the potential plaintiffs and the potential defendants—you need sound legal advice about what to do, what to say, when to say it, and how to proceed.

Physical Plant/Facilities Manager

The physical plant manager may quite literally hold the keys to the kingdom. He or she may best know the design of your facility, the physical security considerations necessary to protect it, the weak points, the safest areas, and how the building(s) may respond to the impact of natural or man-made disasters, from fires to floods to earthquakes or snowstorms.

This person should be cognizant of fire laws, hazardous materials issues, and all the other related compliance regulations that come into play whenever people and buildings come together. The facilities manager may have access to other outside experts: hazardous materials cleanup crews, alarm and fire services experts, janitorial services, locksmiths, etc.

Director of Risk Management

While this position is optional and is usually confined to large city and county municipality staffs, some big firms also employ a person whose sole job it is to manage the risk that comes with running a business. He or she is usually responsible for creating and using risk surveys, dealing with issues relating to business and medical insurance policies, and handling claims made from inside or outside the firm.

Before problems arise, the risk manager can help the rest of the team recognize and respond to issues, events, and conditions related to company or employee liability. During a crisis, he or she can act as a liaison with insurance carriers or help to discuss related risk issues if the firm is self-insured.

Director of Labor Relations

This position is also optional; however, in organizations with a strong union presence, the labor relations director's role is critical to the ongoing operations of the company even before any labor stoppages occur. This key member should already have a finger on the company's union pulse and can offer valuable intelligence information to the entire team should a labor problem develop.

Director of Corporate Communications

This critical position requires iron nerves and the ability to shine under a harsh spotlight. As with some of the other team roles, the communications director may go along his or her way for many months or even years without having to deal with too much corporate turmoil. But like firefighters during the brush fire season, corporate communications directors earn their pay when the going gets hot.

This person will be called upon to gather as much information as possible about a crisis-related incident, write cogent press releases, and communicate a single message to the media and to the public (i.e., "This is our position about what has happened.").

The next two chapters will discuss the criticality of this role in more detail. As a member of the crisis response team, this person will be asked to shoulder much responsibility in terms of carefully managing the company's image, reputation, and position. The position calls for media savvy and a head for appropriate business communications.

Any or all of these positions may be entirely different in your organization. You may have different job titles or a different hierarchical arrangement, such as general managers, department heads, manager of X, or deputy director of Y. The point is, look at your senior people and consider first who should be a permanent member of any crisis response team, and second, how they should best be used.

Allies: Getting Subordinate or Outside Help

Don't forget that the number-two person in charge in each of the above departments also should be a part of the crisis response team—if not actually present in the initial meetings, at least briefed about them afterward. In the rare case that one of the directors is incapacitated (death, sickness, injury) or out of town, the second-in-command can step into his or her shoes.

This leads to the logical and necessary decision to create written plans, policies, and procedures that are germane to the team's collective response and then to the individual director's roles and duties.

As an example, the team could create an emergency policy notebook to explain each member's overall role. If this plan is followed, each department head or director should have separate pages to go along with the notebook. The number-two person in the HR department should know that in the event of an incident where, say, the director of HRD could not respond, he or she is to pull the book, review the respective duties, and initiate them.

But what if you run or manage a *small* business and don't have all these in-house people to fulfil these various important roles? How do you staff a crisis management team with not only limited resources, but limited staff? Here, one person may have to take on a variety of similar or dissimilar duties. And what might already be a part of a big firm, must be hired out by a smaller one. The following are some examples.

A Local Attorney

Many small to midsize firms that do not have in-house counsel keep a law office on retainer. By contracting in this fashion for legal services, they not only save money, but keep an attorney involved in the company's business on a peripheral basis. This avoids the need to locate or reintroduce a new attorney in the event that legal services become suddenly necessary.

Some companies also invite their outside counsel to attend a monthly planning meeting to keep the attorney apprised of any developments that may be significant.

Your Insurance Carrier

The people involved in the insurance side of your firm—the risk managers, benefits managers, etc.—can best make the call as to when and how to include your outside insurance representatives in any planning or crisis response meetings. In a best-case example, the insurance specialists may have some suggestions as to ways to limit your risk, liability, and exposure to certain events or hazards based on their experience with their other clients.

A Public Relations Expert or Media Communications Expert

As with outside legal counsel, some firms keep these kinds of experts on retainer or hire them regularly to draft press releases, make statements for the firm in various public venues, arrange interviews with key company officials, and so forth. Should a crisis situation arise, they will already be familiar with the firm's core message, values, and policies. This ongoing relationship can help them create the most favorable response.

Contract Security Guards

In times of labor strife or to prevent escalating or future security problems, it's not unusual for some companies who do not have an in-house or proprietary security guard force to contract outside with one. The guards may come into the facility during labor flare-ups, strikes, problems with disgruntled or terminated exemployees, or to help handle other people-oriented problems related to the protection of the company.

Help from a Temporary Employment Agency

As in the case of the makers of Similac baby formula (see Chapter 3), sometimes a situation calls for you to put your people and production operations to a tough test. It may be necessary to call in extra help—temporary clerical, semiskilled, skilled, or even management workers to meet new customer or crisis demands.

A Disaster Response Team or Cleanup Crews

This can be a messy job at best and a dangerous one at worst. If you do not have people on staff to help you clean up or dispose of spills, leaks, or other hazardous materials, get qualified help.

In either of these two examples (using inside managers and staff or contracting outside for expert help), any combination of people you can put together will probably suffice; after all, the best you can do is the best you can do. Having a crisis-oriented group in place will get you talking about the problem areas that face your firm.

Crisis Response: A Five-Step Approach

With the team participants in position, it's time to discuss their respective duties, whether working singly or in conjunction with each other.

Step One: Initiate a Risk Assessment Survey

Risk identification is critical to risk avoidance. And although that sounds simplistic and obvious, there are still some company leaders naive enough to believe that their firm has no significant areas of risk, no need for any risk assessment, and no need to create any plans.

During the initial meetings of the crisis response team, the committee members best equipped to audit the organization in terms of risk—the HRD, risk, security, and physical plant managers, for example—should discuss and create an executive-level briefing report that identifies potential areas of loss, vulnerability, and exposure.

The depth and scope of this document will depend upon the size of the firm and the nature of the business. Weighing the probability that something bad will happen to the company, its assets, or its employees is no easy feat. Somc problem areas will be readily apparent; others will require research, observation, interviews with other managers and employees, and even educated guesses to determine.

Step Two: Assign Roles and Discuss Duties

Once they know the company's vulnerabilities and weaknesses and have assessed the potential for addressing them, the crisis response team can meet again to decide the following:

- *Authority.* Who has it? Who provides leadership and direction before, during, and after a significant event that affects the organization? What is the chain of command, especially if top leaders are away or incapacitated?

• *Purpose.* What are the organization's main goals? What are the goals of the crisis response team, before, during, and after a corporate problem that calls them into consideration? Here, the team members should develop a specific mission statement for their representative departments, one that guides them to focus on the protection of life and property, on the protection of business assets, and on legal, ethical, and cost-effective methods to keep the company running. This document can be incorporated with a universal mission statement for the crisis response team.

• *Types of crisis events.* What types of crisis events, natural or man-made disasters, or other physical or psychological emergencies may affect the firm? In what areas is the company most vulnerable? Products? Services? Employees? Materials? Inventory? Image? Customer relationships? Transportation methods? Here, the team needs to look at the way the firm utilizes its various locations, facilities, offices, storage areas, etc. In short, how will the company's people, places, and things be most affected by any accident, crime, civil suit, natural, or man-made disaster? What do the members of the team fear the most? What events do they feel put the organization at the most risk of harm?

• *Implementation instructions.* This is where the committee must make the nuts-and-bolts decisions about how problems will be solved, what resources will be called upon, and who will take what roles—i.e., the who, what, when, where, why, and how of intervention, organizational support, and crisis management. This can include the initial development of internal and external resources, supporting information, phone lists, callback sheets, crisis-specific policies and procedures, etc.

The process of discussing both the problems and missions of the crisis response team is not a one-day, one-meeting event. In some large organizations, it may take weeks or even months to reach a point at which the contingency plans have gone from words to paper. As long as true progress is made with each team meeting, there should be no need to rush the process and thereby create flawed response plans.

Step Three: Respond to the Risk Assessment Report

After the initial risk survey is complete, the team members can begin to focus their efforts on developing loss prevention techniques, risk avoidance strategies, insurance review plans, specific audits of departments, managers, or employees, and other prevention techniques.

This last part is where the group's synergistic effects can be put to good use. Five heads may be better than one, ten heads better than five, etc. Putting the company's divisional or departmental leaders together and asking them to brainstorm on this one area of concern—corporate self-defense—will usually result in a workable set of plans.

Step Four: Write Crisis Response Plans

It's one thing to know what the problem is and it's quite another to know how to solve it. At this stage, the crisis response team must put pen to paper and create a set of operational plans. Suffice it to say, this is not a process that can be finished in an afternoon.

For some companies, creating or rewriting even standard organizational policies and procedures can take months. The typical time frame for the creation of new crisis-related policies can depend upon such factors as the writing skills of the committee participants, the number of times the group can meet, and the availability of all relevant planning, risk management, and other relevant data required to write legal, ethical, and viable procedures.

There are a number of ways to organize a crisis-response policy book. One method is as follows:

- Define specific types of potential crises as they relate to the business.
- Create operational steps to follow for each type of crisis.
- Describe the critical steps necessary to keep the business running during the crisis.
- Determine who would play what role to manage the crisis and keep the business running.

[Planning means the difference between controlling business losses and suffering disasters.]

Step Five: Create an Incident Review Subcommittee

Any time the organization faces a significant problem—a product recall, a trucking accident, a lawsuit, a strike—and handles it to closure, there must be an after-action review of both the incident and the steps taken to solve it. This postmortem period is critical if you want to avoid making the same mistakes again should the problem, or a derivative, flare up later.

To avoid looking back at the encounter is to risk not learning the lessons it teaches. As part of the crisis response team, there should be a separate subcommittee that serves as the "Monday-morning quarterback" for the way problems were handled—whether correctly or not. We learn more from our mistakes than we do from our triumphs.

In any review of past incidents, this subcommittee should be ready to discuss, or put on paper, their recommendations and suggestions for future use. Then the entire group can discuss its findings with an eye toward the betterment of both the company and the committee.

Since it's next to impossible to predict when, where, or why a problem may hit the organization, the group might as well have everything in place beforehand. It's always hard to do the work, but it's always rewarding to see that the efforts at contingency planning will pay off in a pinch.

The APTRA Approach

I have always held the rock-solid belief that

[There is a time to energize and go forward and a time to retreat and regroup; but there is never a good time to sit and wait for bad things to get better.]

Military generals all agree: even a lousy plan is better than no plan at all. Action and reaction should be what guides you, not vague hopes of a miraculous recovery, paralysis, apathy based on fear or ignorance, or any sense that you can or should try to outlast your serious problems without help.

The following acronym—APTRA—is the cornerstone of this book. In its complete form, following vigorous work on your part to match it to the needs of your company, it will serve you during those times that seek to shake the foundations of your firm.

Since there is always more safety in simplicity than complexity, I offer the following crisis management defense plan:

APTRA

1. Anticipate
2. Plan
3. Train and practice
4. Review
5. Act (react, adjust, and move forward)

If this were a perfect world, these five steps (illustrated in Figure 6-1) would solve all our problems and help us manage and cover all our business crises with aplomb and wisdom. Unfortunately, stuff happens. No matter what problem faces your organization, no matter what the size or complexity of the event or episode, and no matter how hard you work to follow these steps, something still may go horribly wrong. The key to your success during any difficult moment lies in your never giving up and never giving in. Better to put some plan of yours into immediate action and follow it than to flail around with nothing to do and nowhere to go.

The APTRA Method for Crisis Management and Incident Control

The ideas expressed in this model are, for the most part, universal to most organizations. Neither the size of your firm nor the number of your executives, managers, supervisors, or employees, neither the type of products or services you sell, nor

Figure 6-1. The APTRA model.

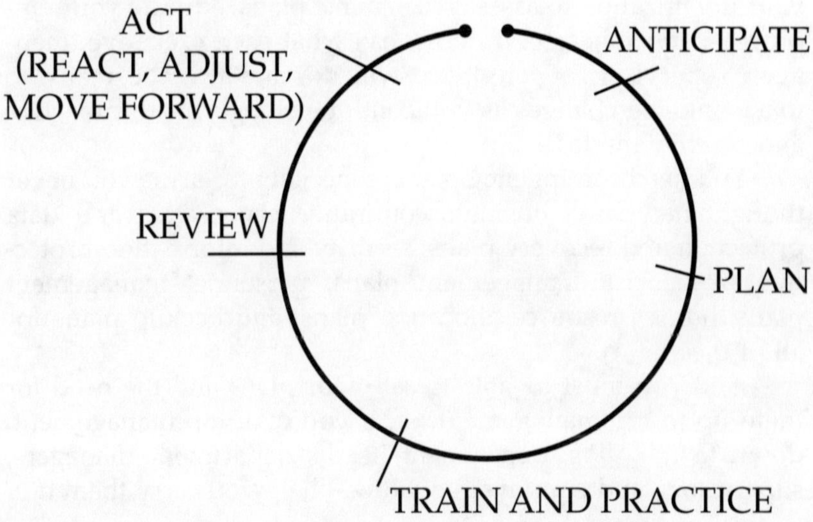

Source: © 1996 Albrecht Training & Development.

your location, industry, or marketplace should keep you from using this model to formulate future response plans and objectives. It will work whether you have 20 employees or 2,000.

While certain industries, markets, products, services are inherently risk-intensive (disposing of spent nuclear fuel rods, making pesticides, or building airplanes, trains, and automobiles, etc.), there should be no limit on how you create plans based on a calculated, careful perception of your firm's ongoing liability areas.

Further, decisions that call for your company's actions following crisis-related events or ones fraught with significant liability should not be made alone. If you don't know it by now, you will certainly have to learn it later:

> Effective and company-saving crisis management responses *must* be part of a *group effort.*

Since it seems unlikely you are reading this book as the sole proprietor or only employee of your firm, you must be ready and able to work together with the other key people in your organization to assess risks, make plans, educate your employees, and rehearse, if necessary, what each executive, manager, supervisor, or employee will do, and then be ready to make ongoing changes as you continue along in both proactive and reactive modes.

You need contingency plans, especially for areas you never thought necessary: business continuity plans; asset and data protection and recovery plans; security and information protection plans; risk management plans; personnel management plans; human resource allocation plans; and backup plans for all of these.

And you must be able to sell your plans and the need for them up to top management, or, if you're *in* top management, down to the VP's, department heads, department managers, supervisors, and employees, who will help you carry them out.

Anticipate

Too many leaders in organizations make their decisions in what might be called "the echo of the gunfire"—meaning that they only respond after something has happened to cause them to move. That's not a good time to be thinking about the problem for the first time. Decisions you can make today about something that might happen tomorrow, next week, next year, or, with luck, never, are a lot stronger than decisions you're forced to make in the heat of the moment, when all around you are losing their heads.

Much of your early thinking starts with your ability to move outside your comfort zone for as long as it takes to discuss the issues at hand. Yes, it *is* unpleasant to talk about potential problems with your products. Yes, it *is* difficult to discuss image problems and their need for careful public image management. And yes, it *is* tough to sit down with your fellow managers and supervisors to talk about strikes, theft, sabotage, threats of workplace violence, significant employee behavioral problems, security issues, or other employee-centered difficulties.

These issues serve to take you away from your day-to-day plans and goals, which, for most companies, is to serve your customers with the best products and services you can create.

Plan

"We're fully prepared for almost anything around here," goes much of the conventional wisdom in organizations today. "We don't really have any written policies about crisis events per se, but we're all sharp people and experienced professionals. If anything goes wrong we'll be able to wing it and come up with the right solutions."

Does this sound like anything you've ever heard, either around your office or at other places where you've worked? Since crisis events are rare, sporadic, and unpredictable, it's all too easy and comfortable to take this "we'll get to it when we get to it" viewpoint.

Planning for things, on the other hand, can be time-consuming, tedious, and distracting from other, "more important" tasks that don't involve the health, safety, and viability of the organization. Planning also can dredge up old problems, past flops, weak points, or incidents many executives and managers would just as soon forget.

But good plans make the workplace better, not just for future difficulties or the problem at hand, but for many aspects of organizational life. As one planner puts it, "Things that are good for *one* portion of the organization are often good for the *rest* of it as well. New security measures don't just benefit the Security Department, they help everyone. Better communication methods, response plans, new role definitions, and changing job duties don't just help the specific departments they are designed for, they make all of us better at our jobs."

When you create plans that people can know, review, and offer suggestions and improvements to, it sends a strong message to other employees that says, "We are *very* interested in what goes on around here. We are *very* interested in the ongoing health, safety, and survivability of this company. And we are *very* interested in your ideas, feedback, and suggestions that will help us keep on track."

You start by gathering your sharpest minds. In large-to-midsize companies, this will probably come from your senior vice presidents, related personnel and HRD department heads, the security director, legal counsel, EAP representatives, and labor union stewards and other representatives. In smaller firms, the senior executive staff should meet and be prepared to discuss their functions and roles. In either case, regardless of your company's size, you should be ready to spend as much time and effort as necessary to create workable, feasible plans that don't necessarily cover every single contingency, but do cover the most important ones.

Your plans will certainly depend upon the needs of your company, but all of them should cover ways to protect your most important assets, among them: your employees, cash and financial instruments, data, physical plant and inventory, products and services, customers, goodwill, and reputation.

In any event, how well you respond in the early going sets the stage for your next moves. Your ultimate goal, besides those relating to the safety of all involved, should be to create plans that help you run your business in as close to an uninterrupted manner as possible.

Train and Practice

We have fire drills in business, tornado drills in the Midwest, hurricane drills in Florida, earthquake drills in California, and bomb threat drills, hazardous-material-spillage drills, and a variety of other emergency practice plans that help get our human assets outdoors and to a position of safety. In other words, we train for these natural or physical disasters on a regular basis (or at least we should).

The people who helped to form your firm's plans should also be the ones who put them into practice. Some people think role plays or skills practice is a waste of time. Experience will tell you that the people who say, "Don't worry about me. I'll know what to do when the time comes. I don't need a dry run," are usually the ones who panic first, worst, and longest.

It's okay to find crisis planning and the subsequent practice scenarios uncomfortable. They're not supposed to be fun, they're supposed to train you how to react.

Consider creating the following mock scenarios (and first make sure that absolutely every person in your facility, plant, office or store knows the difference between the real thing and a drill). In each, you should already know who is in charge, whom to call, and when and how to react in a way that protects your company:

- A power failure that lasts for more than one day
- A large industrial accident that has injured some of your workers and killed others
- The public release of a video tape showing two of your employees engaging in criminal or inappropriate behavior (i.e., fixing prices, substituting old parts, driving erratically, smoking marijuana on the job, dumping waste products, sabotaging company materials, machinery, or products)
- A workplace shooting incident involving a former employee
- A hazardous chemical spill that leaks fumes inside your facility and then later, out into the air
- A suicide on company property
- A phone call announcing the crash of one of your company cars, trucks, freight cars, or planes
- A phone call announcing a customer's serious injury after using one of your products
- A media report questioning the safety of one of your products
- The on-site actions of agitators, protesters from outside your company, or labor union activists within your facility who create problems and get news attention
- A media report from a disgruntled employee who claims that racial problems, sexual harassment, drug use, theft, or workplace violence is taking place inside your organization
- The death, kidnapping, or incapacitating injury of your CEO or other key executive

Each of these training events is based on real-life situations that companies have had to face, so your drill practice for them should be equally realistic. You should be able to simulate many of the events needed to practice each one.

Start by setting up a "war room" so that your crisis response team can meet as a group first. Once you're all in place, the designated team members can begin to coordinate your lines of telephone, fax, and modem communication and your best responses to the nature of each problem.

> If you can communicate with the rest of the world, you'll be able to get your message across, stay abreast of developments, and better manage that priceless commodity known as truthful information.

Training in this kind of crisis response drill would be ideal each quarter, helpful biannually, and mandatory at least once per year.

Review

The review process of your crisis plans should cover three distinct areas: an ongoing review of your policies and procedures manual to clarify the rules of your organization and make sure you are staying within legal guidelines; a postincident review of your training and practice procedures following your run-through of one of the mock scenarios listed above (or one of your own design that is more specific to your firm or industry); and a postincident review following any *real* crisis problem or event.

Good companies always review their actions and activities in the aftermath of any serious or significant corporate problem. They ask themselves and each other:

- Did we solve the problem by doing the right things?
- What did we do right?
- What did we do wrong?
- What were our strong points and what were our weak points?
- What surprised us?
- What were we completely prepared for?
- How well did we work, both as individuals, and as a group?

- What was our biggest area of liability?
- How well did we use our management and supervision roles and duties?
- Were there any telephone calls or announcements we forgot to make or should have made?
- How well did we handle the media?
- How well did we communicate our core message to the various interested publics inside and outside the organization?
- Did we protect our employees as well as possible?
- Did we protect the integrity of the company? Our records, hard assets, financial and personnel data?
- How should we adjust our contingency plans for an even better response in the future?

Act (React, Adjust, and Move Forward)

Going back to the idea that even a bad plan is a good plan, I believe there is more strength, power, and control in *action* than in *reaction*. This is not to say you should charge around your company like a maniac, but neither should you be passive and wait for small problems to go away without a push, or for big problems to solve themselves without a strategic attack. Your experience has probably already demonstrated that neither of these things usually happens. In truth, small problems tend to grow into bigger problems and large ones all too often end up as a threat to the lifeblood of the company.

Sometimes the best people to make decisions during difficult times are the ones who sit furthest from the center of them. Fear of the unknown can cripple many otherwise hearty and bold decision makers. While the CEO and his senior staff are embroiled in some controversy, a department head may be able to look at the problem much more objectively and offer amazingly sound advice.

At other times, an outsider may need to look at the problem or chain of events and offer advice from a third-party position. This role could be played by your outside legal counsel, a public relations adviser, a trusted consultant, or another expert who does not work directly for the company. These people may be able to help you stay in an *active* rather than in a *reactive* mode.

[Stay with what works, change what doesn't, and always be ready to think outside the usual boundaries to solve the problem at hand.]

Get as much advice as you can, but measure that advice against your own instincts as to what you think is right and what will work best.

Building Your Crisis-Related Policies and Procedures Manual

Your firm's crisis response plan is created just like a business plan: one page at a time, with your key people providing input and after a careful review of your mission, core values, and goals.

Don't get confused here: your firm's plan should not replace or supersede your existing policies and procedures manual; it should supplement it. The standard policies and procedures manual is what guides your company; the crisis management portion of it serves as adjunct planning and implementation documents to help company leaders think outside the normal envelope and deal with issues that may happen rarely or with such force as to cause serious damage to the organization.

As a case in point, your firm may have some standard written policies and procedures (P&P) about the proper use and storage of proprietary software. This information would be found in the company P&P manual and perhaps in more detail in the security manager's operational guide.

Misuse of proprietary software that results in significant dollar losses, serious customer problems, or other injurious acts (financial crimes, embezzlement, virus plantings) calls for a crisis response. At this point, certain major portions of the company's finances or computer systems may be at serious risk. These situations would call for specific, separate policies and procedures to protect the company, catch the perpetrators, and prevent the problems from happening again.

Think of the written crisis response plans as if they were a fire alarm. Since we don't hear fire alarms every day, the appropriate response to the bells is a review of the specific crisis management-related procedures. The director of information services, the director of security, and the chief operating officer should have copies of these software protection/data security procedures in their offices. It's up to them to pull them out to incorporate them into the crisis response team's manual so they can be put to use.

Here are some suggestions to help the committee members create new crisis-driven policies and procedures that relate to corporate self-defense:

• *Get sound legal advice before you proceed to print hard copies of the crisis response manual.* Once the committee has created crisis-specific P&P pages, the firm's in-house or outside counsel should review them for accuracy, validity, and effectiveness.

What sounds great during a meeting may not read so well once it's written down. Ask the attorneys for advice relating not just to legal issues but to how well the policy or procedure helps the director or the company solve the problem at hand.

• *Keep it simple.* Since the crisis portion of your P&P manual will be stored, read, and acted upon by the various department heads, you don't have to account for every single legal possibility (unless you want your crisis P&P manual to look and carry like a phone book). In most instances, these particular P&P's will *not* be distributed to the rank-and-file employees.

• *Create a secure storage area for the crisis plans in each director's office.* These plans should *not* be stored with the regular P&P manual, but in a more secure location, like a locked file cabinet, a locked desk, or better yet, a small safe. The reason for this added security is clear: it does not make sense to allow employees, outsiders, vendors, customers, or any other people who may have a hidden agenda against the company to see the plans, policies, and procedures for corporate self-defense. Each committee member should do what is necessary to protect this proprietary information. (In other words, professional football teams don't leave their playbooks lying around just anywhere.)

• *Use this crisis-planning opportunity to improve your current P&P manual.* As the crisis response team adds supplemental crisis management P&P pages to the company manual, it should also review the existing employee policies with an eye to adding, deleting, or rewriting them. If you've outgrown your P&P manual, or if it's no longer up to date, you can get help from the many boilerplate software programs on the market.

In Case of Emergency: Take These Three Steps

Groups can be hard to organize and even harder to control. With many agendas and not much time, it can be difficult to stay focused on the issues that count. For the crisis response team concept to work, both individually and as a group, there has to be a commitment to the long-term health of the company. The sooner the members can check their egos at the door and get down to the real issues, questions, and solutions, the stronger the team will become as it grows and develops.

First: Get Organized

Surround yourself with your most important commodity: information.

Second: Think Hard

Put a plan to paper and be ready to ride to the sound of the cannons with it. Make good, solid, legal, and ethical decisions based upon timely information, advanced knowledge of your company's core values, and the right message you want to send as you attempt to lessen the effects of any significant problem.

Third: Act Swiftly

Don't wait for the circumstances to get more favorable. There is no "perfect moment" in which to act. Make the hard choices and go forward with information and action steps—for the sake of your employees, your customers, your shareholders, the media, and all the other publics out there who will be watching what you do.

7

Bright Lights and Cameras

How to Use the Media and Not Let the Media Use You

> The press, the movies, radio and television bear a large share of the responsibility for the climate of fear . . . which has enveloped our country and which has become a threat to our freedom.
>
> —William T. Evjue

Not every problem that hits your organization will be large enough to involve the media. Most events that start in-house can stay in-house. And based on your skills, as well as on the types of products and services your firm sells, it should stay that way. The vast majority of product, image, or employee problems can and should be handled with discretion and tact inside the organization.

So, based on your own assessment of your firm, can you safely and accurately say that for every 10 serious problems that hit your company, perhaps only one will interest the local or national media? If that's true, then you still have your work cut out for you: the one the media covers could be significant to the reputation of your firm. No one ever went into business saying, "Two years from now, one of our products is going to fail and we will have to read all about it in the newspapers," but you must plan for it anyway.

The Coexistence Between the Media and Business

An old joke making the rounds years ago started with the phrase, "You know it's going to be a bad day when you come to work and find Mike Wallace and the *60 Minutes* team in your office." Depending on the work your firm does and your relationship with your customers, employees, the media, and the community around you, this has more truth than humor in it. Only today, it might not be just Mike Wallace and his pals who have brought their cameras and lights to the doorstep of your store, business, or factory; it could be every news station and newspaper in your town, state, or hemisphere.

This chapter begins with the premise, "Just like you, the media has a job to do. If you make it tough on them to file their stories about your incident, they'll make it even tougher on you." As Los Angeles Dodgers manager Tommy Lasorda always says, "Never argue with people who buy their newsprint by the truckload and their ink by the gallon."

> The media can serve as your ally rather than just your enemy. How they treat you throughout any news event involving your firm depends largely upon how you treat them from the start.

The stonewall 'em, no-comment, tight-lipped response only drives media people to dig deeper, and if you give them nothing significant to report, they may create something, which only makes matters worse.

Meet a Media Relations Master

Chet Burchett, senior vice president of Edelman Public Relations Worldwide, has just the kind of background you would like to see in your own PR expert: he used to be a newspaper reporter and editor himself.

One of Burchett's favorite training exercises is to hire former print and TV reporters and bring them into companies where he consults. He begins by setting up role-play press conferences, using various corporate disasters like the ones we have discussed in this book as the backdrop. When he turns the reporters loose on the corporate spokespeople, the results are dramatic, especially after some of the more befuddled managers see a replay of themselves fumbling their answers on videotape. Their education process begins anew.

The results of Burchett's training and guidance are impressive. Corporate employees, faced with a highly public event, can now handle themselves effectively and safely. This chapter presents Burchett's tips on how you can use the media to your best advantage during a significant event. Unless otherwise noted, the quotations throughout the chapter are drawn from an extensive interview with Burchett in Chicago on November 18, 1994.

Communication Cycles: Making the Most of the Clock

Although you always want to evaluate your initial and subsequent positions during any public problem, speed—in terms of your response time—is more your friend than your enemy. Says Burchett:

> Your response during the first couple of news cycles means more than everything that comes after. The way the company initially positions itself, the way they initially respond to the media, and to the public, and to the problem, means more in the first 12 to 48 hours than everything they do over the next two years.

To Burchett, however, this does not mean that you should leap into the fray with an encyclopedia of information for the press. Sometimes, less is better. He says:

> I am a minimalist in crisis communications. I believe that you speak to the issues, you speak candidly, and

> that you take responsibility and accountability for your organization. You have to communicate clearly what your messages are, but you don't communicate to a point where you suddenly begin driving the issue. Ultimately, in a crisis, you'd like the problem to go away and get back to business.

If you'll recall the Snapple case from Chapter 4, the beverage company took out ads in various national newspapers to defend its position. The ads carefully explained that the K (for kosher) on the Snapple label had absolutely, positively nothing to do with the KKK and that the scene on the bottles depicted the Boston Tea Party. Were they well served by these ads? Clearly they worked. The question of racism at Snapple quickly became a nonissue.

Would they have been equally well served by ignoring the growing controversy and letting the problem solve itself? Perhaps, but small problems have an irritating way of becoming big ones, especially if you wait for them to fix themselves.

According to Burchett, in any perception problem relating to your company, you have two initial responses: (1) admit that the perceptions may be true and agree to make changes; or (2) disagree and don't. Which action you take depends upon a number of factors (with the costs involved being the primary one) but it should be a logical decision based upon thought and research, not a spur-of-the-moment leap that sends you in the wrong direction. Burchett puts it this way:

> A lot of problems occur because people don't communicate very well up front and they immediately become defensive. They try to blow off the issue as no big deal or something insignificant. Anytime somebody makes a case against you, as in a lawsuit, no matter what the plaintiff claims, you have to give it your attention and consider it. You can bet the media will, and the public will pick up on it and may not understand all the issues. One of the core issues for the media is *conflict*.

Since little things can snowball into big things, it's important for you not to be trapped in a constant-catch-up position. What are your communication options, in the earliest stages of a business problem in which the media is fast becoming interested? Let's review them:

- Do nothing.
- Write an open letter to the newspapers and try to get them to publish it. (Or pay for the ad space yourself.)
- Write a letter to the injured parties (if there are any yet), explain your position, and invite them to meet with you to discuss the problem.
- Call a national or local reporter and give your side of the issue.
- Call a local press conference to address the issue, make a clarifying statement, and answer questions.
- Call a national press conference to address the issue, make a clarifying statement, and answer questions.

One or more of these options may serve your best interests in the early stages of a controversy. Which ones you choose will depend upon many factors, but the list gives you a broad spectrum to choose from.

Indirect Impact Versus Direct Impact: The End User Bears the Yoke

If your company manufactures or sells only one thing—granola bars, say—and somehow, despite your every precaution, a pile of broken glass gets into a production run of 10,000 bars and these tainted snacks are blanketed across the country by your distributors, you have an obvious product problem.

Once the word gets out—as unwary consumers begin cutting their mouths, slashing their small intestines, or otherwise ending up sick, injured, or dead—there is a *direct impact* on your bottom line and, ultimately, on the survivability of your company. If you can't sell granola bars, you're out of business.

While this may appear painfully obvious, the distinction becomes less clear if you change the scenario to a more *indirect impact.* Say, for example, that your firm mills the oats and other grains used to make granola bars for other snack manufacturers across the country. You sell bags and bags of the raw ingredients to granola bar companies from Portland, Oregon, to Portland, Maine. Now, if a tainted product problem erupts, what is your level of exposure?

In the first place, you're removed from the consumer who buys granola bars at the store. Your products are not necessarily (or immediately) associated with the tainted end product.

What makes this connection-by-extention to tainted products is how well you manage the event on your side of the fence. In effect, you need to "shadow" the efforts of the granola bar company at fault, using your own public relations strategies and recovery plans so that, should your company's name reach the light of day, you're prepared with hard data that says:

> *We stand behind the safety, sanctity, and quality of our oats and grains one hundred percent. Our milling and production processes are state-of-the-art and meet or often exceed industry standards. We know our raw products reached the granola bar factories intact and untainted. Here are our inspection and delivery reports to prove it. The fault, unfortunately, for all concerned, and especially for the injured consumers, lies in the way these bars were created by the granola bar firm.*

But what is the future impact of a seemingly insurmountable press problem? What might happen to your profits if the press plays pitch-and-catch with your company? In real terms, maybe nothing. Few people recall that Exxon had record profits the next year after the *Valdez* oil spill. Chet Burchett addresses the importance of your image:

> When consumer confidence in your product disappears, *you're lost.* And when a crisis strikes at your credibility or your veracity as an organization, it's doubly bad. Your normal channels of marketing communication—advertising and such—are taken away from you as an advantage in restoring consumer confidence. If they lose trust in you, you're going to have a hard time gaining trust via the typical means of communicating.

When Media Channels Turn Ugly: The Dangers of the "No Comment" Mantra

What happens when the media serves as a negative channel of information about your firm? How do you cope when Dan Rather, Peter Jennings, or Tom Brokaw starts his newscast with a story about your company that makes it seem as though it's suddenly two baby steps from insolvency?

Here, you can't immediately defend yourself (since Dan, Peter, or Tom don't take calls during their newscasts). When the media begins trying your product, image, legal, or public relations case for you, it's time to get up and do something about it.

Chet Burchett suggests that no matter what the size of your company or the size of your problem, you must be ready to work with the media in good times and in bad. Waiting for them to make your decisions for you is like waiting for the judge to dismiss a lawsuit against you without showing up to provide reasons or a reasonable defense; it could happen, but you wouldn't want to bet on it. He defines the media's role and function:

> Public communication about your company through the media provides a third-party delivery of your message and, more important, an implied credibility to what you're saying. It gives outsiders the impression that they've looked into your affairs and that

> what you say must somehow be viable. Certainly a positive story in the media is held in a higher degree of respect than some advertisement created by the company.

He continues this thought:

> In any significant crisis, the media is your primary communication device with a broad public. But they certainly aren't the only one, and the mistake people make often times is that they depend solely on the media to communicate with the audiences they've got to talk to. Or they retreat from the media, thinking if they don't talk to them they can hold the line.
>
> The bottom line in a crisis is that somebody is going to talk for your company. If you don't, somebody will. Probably it will be somebody from the opposition, people from the other side of the crisis, or the media, in a detached manner.
>
> To say "No comment," in this day and age, is just unforgivable. There is a difference between not responding and not commenting. "No comment" doesn't mean that the company isn't making a statement.

Companies that always want to stick to the "No comment" method of media relations have, in effect, opened the floodgates and let the waters flow. Burchett is quick to say that there is a fine balance point with the media between not enough help and too much:

> There are instances when not providing comment is perfectly rational, especially in terms of detail. But there are very few instances where a company doesn't have any kind of a response. You should always respond. You don't necessarily answer everything in detail because certainly there are things it is not in your best interest to discuss. But by its nature

> the company has a position to take, and if the leaders don't advocate that position, nobody else will.

Putting on Your Brave Face Early: Organizing Your Primary and Secondary Issues

Like many crisis management experts, Burchett suggest you get your ducks in a row long before any event strikes. This includes doing some careful planning, looking at issues, putting together a crisis management response team, and developing a set of core messages:

> You have to decide up front what you're going to do. You have to step back and decide things like: Who is your audience? What is the issue? And the issue that you establish as important is not always the one that gets covered. There's a difference, and this is a mistake a lot of companies make.

Here's an example of what can happen when organizations take a canted, one-sided look at a serious corporate problem:

Let's say your firm manufacturers products like chemicals, pesticides, or nuclear or biological materials that are under strict federal control. If there is a significant leak, spill, or accident at your facility, the *primary* issues are: the potential impact upon the surrounding community; the health and safety of your employees; and the perception of safety and reliability by your local citizens and customers. A *secondary* issue is whether or not your firm will be criticized by the government and found to be at fault. Other secondary issues include: how fast you can get back to full production; how quickly you can fill customers' orders and ship their products; or how and when you can conduct a complete safety check of all your operating, disposal, safety, and production systems.

Of these two types of issues—primary and secondary—too many toxic-products companies worry about the latter over the former. The main problem lies not in the government's perception of whether you followed their rule book to the letter or whether you were operating in a manner that paralleled federal guidelines. The main problem following a toxic accident to be faced is: Is this building now safe? Is this community now safe? Are the citizens and our employees now safe? Have we done everything physically possible to ensure that the answers to these questions are now true?

Here we see the difference between the primary *corporate* issues (Will we be sued? How fast can we get back to work? What, if any, impact will this have on our stock price, customers, or shareholder's confidences?) and the primary *public* issues (Are we safe? Has everything possible been done to care for all the people involved in this event?)

As Burchett puts it:

> In these kinds of incidents the public cares about safety. They don't care about federal compliance guidelines, or who was right or wrong, or whose fault anything was. Companies who can focus on the public will be in a better position to take actions that are in the public interest. They can start to rehabilitate their image, facilitate government relations, and carry them on forward and beyond the event. If they continue to fight what they think the issue is—the government's reaction—they can get mired in one place and go nowhere.

The Need to Let Go: Objectivity From the Start

Once you've determined the primary and secondary issues, says Burchett, you've got to be willing to divorce yourself from your own position:

> Look at things from the position of the people on the other side of the crisis. You need to really look at their position and look for the validity of that position. Don't dismiss it. Take a really candid look at it.

> The hardest thing to do in the heat of the moment is to stand back and objectively look at your organization. This is the reason you need to have already done a lot of advance planning, especially with any area where you might have some exposure.

What makes this necessary search for objectivity so difficult becomes readily apparent when the CEO's own ego is tied up in the proceedings.

> When a company problem becomes public, it's always hard for the leader to keep a civil tongue, especially in the earliest stages, when everyone from the media to customers and from employees to boards of directors is clamoring for more information about what happened and why. These times call for CEOs who spend more time thinking, planning, and reacting and less time talking.

Chet Burchett recalls a case in which his firm was called in by an organization to do some issues-preparedness planning. The company had no immediate risk-related problems. The leaders just wanted to see what kind of exposure they faced in various parts of the organization. In short, management was asking, "Where are we at risk, in terms of our products and services?"

By the end of their study however, the PR team came back to top management with issues that had not even been on its original agenda. During the focus groups and individual employee interviews the team conducted to uncover liability issues relating to specific products, a more startling finding had surfaced relating to the company's equal employment opportunities. In a sentence, too few minority employees were in positions of authority, supervision, and management. And in looking at the numbers involved in this personnel issue, it became clear that the company was at significant risk of exposure with regard to its minority hiring, promoting, and affirmative action policies.

While this was not the initial focus of the organizational survey, it suddenly went to the top of the CEO's list as a liability issue. The company's belief that it might have product liability problems was overshadowed by the fact that it had few minority employees in positions of authority and no active mentoring programs. As such, the firm was ripe for a discrimination suit and public condemnation.

To the company's credit, it dealt with this issue swiftly and with a strong sense of purpose. Top management immediately created a minority training program, a management mentoring program, and an active program from within the company to recognize, recruit, and promote qualified minority employees into management and supervision positions.

All of this came about without the need for corporate attorneys to shout at the company, without the onus of a lawsuit over the firm's collective head, and prior to any event brought on by this initial flaw in their HR policies.

Good thing too, because within six months, the company *was* sued for an EEO violation. But because it had already put a program in place, because it had addressed the issue previously from a worst-case-scenario standpoint, and because it had done plenty of advanced planning and preparation for the inevitability of an employee civil suit, it wasn't surprised or caught off guard when it appeared.

Chet Burchett points to the company's defense as multifaceted:

> Their initial position in response to the suit was that the current management team had inherited some of these problems, and they said. "We don't believe we are where we need to be on this issue. That's why we've instituted EEO programs now and in the past. This is what our plan is, and this is where we're going on this issue." That was their public representation. They still got sued, but what they took away was the public "bludgeon" that they were a "whitebread" organization that didn't care about its employees. That was solely because they had recognized it up front and had taken a detached "outsiders" look at their organization. And then, because they weren't under fire, they had the freedom to re-

ally ask themselves, "What do we stand for? What do we need to do? What's the right thing to do in this situation?" They knew and they did it.

The Myth of the Episodic Crisis

The main objection to the need for preproblem planning is universal, regardless of what episode or possible catastrophe may ever plague your organization. It starts and ends with the insistence that most significant company problems are episodic—i.e., "We don't have that kind of problem here, we haven't had that problem in the past, and we don't anticipate having that problem in the future."

PR expert Chet Burchett puts it this way:

> If you are involved in commerce today, if you are a company of some size—and certainly as you get bigger the degree of risk grows—if you sell something to the public, if you manufacture something, if you employ people, you face an issues-management potential. You can ignore it. You can say, "There's no reason for me to spend money right now. Resources are tight, bottom lines are low. I'm not going to spend the money on planning because it's not a problem today. I'm going to focus on other problems today." You're putting your company at risk, and when a problem *does* occur, it will cause you more damage and cost you more money, and in the long term, it will be more debilitating, financially and emotionally, than preparing for it ever would be.

Consider the further advantages as he describes them:

> Prior planning lowers organizational stress. It allows consensus. It allows people to talk about issues, and ultimately, can head off a future problem. A lot of

> crisis planning is in prevention. It's in noticing there are existing problems. It's asking the right questions. It's answering the questions that say, "We're in compliance with regulations, but is that the right thing? Have we looked at our company's operations in terms of the potential exposures?" Crisis planning is all about weighing and reducing the odds.

Clearly, you won't be able to solve every single issue; some things will be out of your control. If you've identified potential problems A, B, and C, and you can only actively control C, then at least you've recognized the existence of all three in the first place. No one expects you to be clairvoyant. Crisis management is not about *predicting* the future, it's about *reacting* to it in a planned, prepared, thoughtful, and aggressive manner.

The "Public": More Than You Might at First Think

Various audiences or publics, each with different or similar agendas, will watch your performance with a highly critical eye. Burchett discusses this:

> Companies get into problems during a crisis when they fight the public interest. And in many cases, the "publics" are different. They may be customers, employees, investors, suppliers, business associates, and the media. The media is more of a conduit, but they need to be treated as a separate public, audience. Each of these people have a different agenda. Each of those people have a different core interest. For the employee, it may be, "Am I going to lose my job?" For the vendor or the customer it may be, "Am I going to lose business?" For the financial partner, it may be, "Am I going to get burned on this?" And for the consumer, it might be, "Am I going to lose my life by using this product?"

Honest, open, timely, and forthright communication is the key to both your early stability and your later success. What these different groups need to hear from you is a message, in the midst of a problem, that addresses each of their interests. That's why "no comment" doesn't work.

Answering by Not Answering: The Hidden Power of Bridging

> Your core messages during any difficult, publicized event should serve as your road map for how to respond to any public scrutiny—ranging from general to intense. These core messages—and there should be no more than three or four—will help you stay on track.

Armed with these principles and some supporting data, you can be better equipped to handle questions.

If you don't know where you're going, you can't possibly get there. In press conferences and telephone interviews, it's easy to start talking about other side issues, or worse, to get drawn into areas you should for the most part avoid. This is especially hazardous during question-and-answer sessions, that often cause untrained company representatives to start answering questions they are neither prepared for, trained for, or qualified to answer.

The pitfalls that many untrained or unprepared corporate executives face start when they try to freewheel up at the lectern. People inside the organization who are unfamiliar with media relations need to know how to "bridge" their answers back to areas where they are more comfortable. Most politicians are masters at the art of bridging. When asked a seemingly tough question designed to make them look bad or worse, they can sidestep the question they don't like and provide an answer that better serves their purpose.

This is a learned skill but not an excessively difficult one to practice and master. Here's a short example to demonstrate its power. As you review this passage, notice how the interviewer attempts to bait the executive into a trap:

Reporter: Ms. Jones, is it your company's policy to allow tainted granola bars on to the market?

Ms. Jones: Of course not. What's important in this case is that our production procedures are well-supervised and thorough. We've taken great care on our end to make sure our products cannot be tampered with before, during, or after the production run.

Reporter: But in this case, two people in Missouri ate your granola bars and got sick from them. Doesn't that mean that you should pull the product off the shelves all across the country?

Ms. Jones: We are, of course, deeply concerned about the health of our customers in Missouri. We're asking hard questions about the quality of our product in those two specific cases. We've contacted the customers and have agreed to pay for their medical bills for their treatment.

Reporter: But what about initiating a complete product recall?

Ms. Jones: We stand behind our products and our production processes. Our quality control procedures go above and beyond the industry standards. We do random taste tests every day and we follow up at our storage warehouses to make sure the products are sealed and tamper-proof prior to shipping.

Reporter: So are you saying you're not going to recall all your bars? Isn't that putting the whole country at risk?

Ms. Jones: Because we keep careful track of every granola bar we make, there is a production control number stamped on every box. Because of this, we know exactly which boxes went to the store in Missouri and we have already replaced them. We've sent the granola bars in question to an independent testing lab for study. We will have the input of that study in about three days and, of course, I'll call you with the results so you can add them to your story.

This exchange has taken place in the perfect world of a business book, of course, but the principles of bridging are the same regardless of the subject or the nature of the inquiry. As you can see from the conversation, the inquirer wanted to get the executive to admit that *all* of the granola bars were tainted. Knowing that this was not true, the executive refused to be baited into making blanket statements about the safety of all the bars on the market.

Each time he tried to steer the issue back to a total recall, the executive reminded him of the high-quality production processes used to make the bars. Production integrity became the executive's theme, and she bridged over to it every time. This is the same tack *Nightline* host Ted Koppel took with Pepsi CEO Craig Weatherup (i.e., "In light of finding these syringes in Pepsi cans, shouldn't you recall the product from our shelves?"). Weatherup didn't fall for it. He carefully explained that he and his company believed these were aberrant incidents of postproduction product tampering. He saw no need to recall his product and made an honest and convincing argument in favor of his position.

Prior PR and Media Planning

Money is always a significant factor in every business decision you make. The ways you spend your money on crisis management support is more a necessary cost of doing business in the 1990s than an expense.

When the media comes calling, they will want hard facts, figures, numbers behind the people, and people behind the numbers. If you have nothing in place right now, start with a media "audit": an outline that looks at your risks, liabilities, assets, exposures, and security risks from their point of view. What questions might the media ask about your firm, and how will you answer them? Consider, as well, the following equally difficult questions:

- Who is the primary media spokesperson? Who is the secondary media spokesperson? If it is the CEO, who will speak for us if the CEO or his designated replacement is incapacitated or unavailable? What kind of media training have they had? When do they get it, who gets it, and who conducts it?

Some outside PR companies or other consultants begin by teaching the chief executive the basics of good media relations, press release creation, and information management. Then they put the executive to the ultimate test by bringing in one or more news reporters to stage a mock news conference.

- What are your basic, essential, core messages?

  Start by creating and storing press kits, background materials, and fact sheets on the company, safety and performance issues (these should be updated on a regular basis anyway). You need to have this material in hand so that you can open a dialogue with your various publics: the media, your customers, consumers, stockholders, and other interested parties.

Chet Burchett comments on media management themes:

Reporters will make a decision early on in any story as to whether or not you and your spokespeople are a viable, primary source of information. You establish that relationship by being open on as many issues as feasible. While you can't comment on everything, you can say, "I really can't tell you everything right now because we're still gathering facts. What I can tell you is this: Here's some information on the company, here's some background on our safety record, manufacturing processes, procurement, or whatever it might be." When you begin to feed them some information, you've given them something to work with. When you help them do their story well, they'll be more prone to come back to you to ask for more information.

The best thing a company can do in times of crisis is to establish *itself* as the *primary* source of information about the company and the problem. If you

> don't, the media will go and talk to the guy standing next to the fire truck, the contractor hired by the state, the regulatory officials, or the activists. But they're not going to be talking to you and it's *your* problem.

Speak the Truth

Chet Burchett offers a crucial piece of advice: *Don't lie!* If something bad happens to or at your company, don't sugarcoat it, or worse, call it something it's not. Stay away from euphemisms that try to make a bad thing better. A nuclear power plant meltdown is not "an unanticipated release of minute radioactivity." A raging fire in and around your factory is not a "small blaze," when half the city can see the glow from their front porches. Burchett is firm here:

> Speaking the truth doesn't mean that you just go out and answer every question and open the books. That's not necessarily in your best interest. It means never saying anything that's not the truth. The biggest mistake that people make happens when they're trying to be helpful and they tell the media something they believe is true. They're not sure, but they *think* it's true. It gets reported as fact; it's wrong; and now the company is a liar and they've lost credibility. In a time of crisis, it's critical to plan ahead of time and get your facts straight before you say anything.

Always remember that it's you or your company spokespeople who should ultimately control the information about any event—positive or negative—taking place in, near, or because of your firm. Treat the media with respect, but demand it in return. Be fair and ethical, and if you decide to give any statement, make it an honest one right from the start.

8

Positive Corporate Public Relations

PR as an Offensive and Defensive Weapon

> Before the beginning of great brilliance, there must be chaos. Before a brilliant person begins something great, they must look foolish to the crowd.
>
> —from the *I Ching*

Positive public relations is not about some sharply dressed "mouthpiece" who smiles and offers the company party line each time a hard question is raised. Rather, it's about the ethical, honest, and useful release of information to the outside publics who want to know more about what has happened and what will happen in your organization.

Several highly publicized corporate crises became worse, not better, because company spokespeople did not understand the dynamics of positive PR. Where the preceding chapter focused on your firm's relationship with the media, this one looks at the value to a specific public relations strategy. As with most image management tools, the time to develop your PR mission is before you really need one.

Organizations that have a history of bad feelings between groups—i.e., law enforcement, government, big and unfeeling conglomerates, natural resource companies that mine or harvest their raw materials—come into any highly public event with one hand already tied. The key to positive PR is, first to admit that this gap exists, and then to seek to close it with honest attempts to discuss your actions or the perception of your actions.

The Tylenol Success Model: Doing the Right Things the Right Ways

Portions of this book have focused on the negative side of corporate self-defense—that is, what companies did wrong after something or someone did them wrong. Just as it's beneficial to learn from past mistakes, it makes sense from a PR perspective to examine how certain firms did things *correctly* from step one to closure. Let's look at the right way to respond to a building public relations problem, using Johnson & Johnson's actions during and after the Tylenol problem. The firm and its leaders:

- Fully admitted to the problem when it first surfaced
- Accepted fault and didn't hide behind the problem or try to affix the blame on someone or something else
- Made the right public decision to remove or recall the product and changed the policies and procedures that caused or allowed to cause the problem in the first place
- Came out with a safer, improved product, made the right organizational changes in personnel and production, and told the public what they did to make things right

In the case that follows, we will see an organization and its leader who failed on each of these four counts. The results were disastrous, and not just from a dollars standpoint, but from a PR one as well. Even today, this organization continues to fight for the smallest modicum of respect from the public it is supposed to protect and serve.

Rodney King Versus Daryl Gates: The Winner Gets Los Angeles

In reviewing the events that took place on a cool night in Los Angeles on March 3, 1991, it's safe to say that the videotaped arrest and assault of Rodney King by several Los Angeles police officers stands as one of the most-watched TV events of the past decade.

Thanks to this sweeping exposure, worldwide access, and countless repetitions of the video incident, the Los Angeles Police Department has spent the past five years defending its image and police practices, not just in the American court of public opinion, but in the international one as well. (And thanks to the divisive testimony of LAPD Detective Mark Fuhrman during the 1995 O. J. Simpson trial, this image-polishing process will have to begin anew.)

Angry riots erupted in Los Angeles after the trial of the police officers involved in King's beating. By the time the last looters, rioters, and arsonists had been locked up, the second-largest city in America had been successfully shut down, held hostage, and damaged by a relatively small number of its riled-up citizens. Together, the Rodney King video, officer court trials, riots, and civil damages suits delivered a severe and long-lasting black eye to the entire city. If things had been handled properly from the beginning—if the right message had been sent to the public, the media, and the citizens of Los Angeles—we would not have seen anything like the disastrous results that ensued. It offers us a classic study of what *not* to do in a crisis.

Engaging in "Gates-Speak": A Lesson in What Not to Say

Sometimes in life, there's what's right and there's what's almost right. The first media management rule of thumb is always the same: "In times of corporate trouble, have the CEO step forward into the limelight, give a statement, and take the questions."

The reasoning for this has always been abundantly clear: People want to hear from the person in charge. They want to see a buck-stops-here approach, and be assured that the leader is visible, in control, and ready to handle the consequences of the event. Give us information, possible solutions, and some measure of hope, especially if what has happened impacts a large number of us, makes us worry about our future safety, or stands in the way of the organization's credibility and recovery.

In the wake of the Rodney King videotape arrest, Los Angeles Police Chief Daryl Gates was *not* the right man for this job. Here we had a leader of one of the largest metropolitan police departments in the nation, full of bluster and outrage, and communicating, *not* the message of his organization, but his own personal feelings.

In the days following the Rodney King incident, Gates, ever the blame-monger, stepped onto the podium in front of a LAPD Academy graduating class, and with the eyes of the world upon him, proceeded to announce that he would serve as judge, jury, and executioner of the police officers involved in the incident:

> A few thoughtless officers [who] failed to have a reverence for the law . . . failed to understand their job to protect and to serve . . . failed the tradition and pride of the Los Angeles Police Department.[1]

Later, in a videotape sent to all LAPD patrol commands, Gates made it crystal clear that he was in charge:

> When I say that my way is the way it is going to be, then that's the way it's going to be. I assure you that anyone who questions what I have to say—and questions it in any way—and demonstrates that in any manner, or chooses to disagree in some kind of action—that they will rue the day that they have disagreed with what I have to say.[2]

In one swift movement, Gates succeeded in alienating his cops forever. Instead of saying that he wanted to investigate the events thoroughly and that he would like the cooperation of everyone, he used veiled threats to make his point. The die had been cast; now that the rank-and-file officers knew their leader's position, they had two choices: join with him or be ostracized. In the beginning, many took the first choice, but once the riots were in full eruption, most chose their own path and abandoned Gates at a time when he could most have used their support.

What should he have said? The possibilities should have been narrowed to three choices: What is the right thing to say to the public, using the media? What is the appropriate response from our organization, not just my own point of view? And what message will serve our interests without appearing to be a cover-up, a stonewalling, or any other insensitive handling of the events nearly everyone in the world has already seen?

Gates *could* have gathered an assembly of reporters and gave them the following statement:

> *We're deeply shocked by the events caught on tape. Clearly, this arrest process went beyond our formal procedures and did not follow our training methods. I will launch a complete investigation into this incident and we will get a complete reckoning of the events. I expect each of the officers involved to cooperate fully with this investigation, as well as all the other members of this police department. Once our investigation is complete, I will decide upon the appropriate disciplinary actions for the people involved. Until then, I think it's important for the people of this city to know this is not the usual way we conduct ourselves in the streets. It's my deep hope that this shocking incident will not jeopardize the relationship between the LAPD and the citizens of this city.*

He did not. When pressed, Gates retreated into two modes: the typical stern-faced "no comment" that has damaged everyone who has tried to use it, and the "I'm right and I'm in charge, so the hell with all the rest of you" approach. With these as his only methods of communicating the LAPD message to the media and the public, it's not surprising that some angry people took to the streets.

Know Your Audiences!

In terms of reaching (or failing to reach) his various audiences, Gates's remarks deserve study from a number of angles, especially in light of the various "publics" involved. Clearly, Gates's eyes were focused on saving his own bacon first, his department's second, and everyone else's afterwards. In hindsight, he failed to address the worries, concerns, needs, interests, and demands of the following groups:

- The police officers involved in the King incident
- The Los Angeles Police Department rank-and-file officers
- The media
- Minority rights groups
- The mayor's office and city council members
- The investigators sent in by the federal government to examine the events
- The citizens of Los Angeles as a whole

Did Daryl Gates ever gear his public messages to address the needs or concerns of these groups separately and then together? No. Instead he started with the premise that said: "What will make Daryl Gates look good? What will keep Mayor Tom Bradley's office off my neck? And what will make the media think that I'm doing my job, even though I would rather have dental surgery with posthole diggers than speak to them?"

Most of Gates's problems in communicating—with the public, with the media, and with his officers—came about as a result of his nature. He had come up through the ranks quickly, not via street patrol, which would have endeared him to the rank-and-file officers. He was as a driver for LA Police Chief William Parker in the 1960s, then later, a desk jockey. His rise to command ranks, many veteran LAPD officers argued, was because he was a consummate politician.

In his book *Presumed Guilty,* which details his on-scene involvement in the Rodney King incident, Sergeant Stacey Koon puts it this way:

> The fact is this: Chief Daryl Gates is, or was, at least, a good politician in his time. He knew how to work the system to protect Daryl Gates and his command staff. So when things went wrong, the street cops got

> screwed, as we knew we would be, while the big guys got protected. It was the LAPD double standard at work.[3]

Gates was a product of 1960s policing methods, and his management and leadership style reflected his immersion in a time that included the Watts riots, the assassinations of several of our political and civil rights leaders, and a general sense that the establishment—and thereby, the police—was out to kick butts and take names, especially if you were a minority.

The problem was that as the years progressed from the 1960s to the present day, the national and Los Angeles public no longer bought into the us-versus-them policing concept. By the 1980s and 1990s they were ready to work with their police agencies to fight crime together. Gates was not ready to believe that the public and the police could ever work together.

Mixing his hard-core philosophy with his role as politico, Gates ruled his domain with little flexibility, poor communication skills with the outside world, and a management style that said that everybody, cops included, had better toe his line.

Sergeant Stacey Koon summarizes Gates's response to the King incident this way:

> When the Rodney King incident got hot, Gates had to make a choice. He could stand up and back his officers, or he could waffle and protect himself from an increasingly hostile assault from his worst enemy, Mayor Tom Bradley. If Gates chose right, his street cops would follow him through the seven gates of hell. If he chose wrong, his officers would abandon him and he would lose his strongest base of support. Gates made the wrong choice. And the street cops turned their backs on him. That was when his departure from the LAPD was certain, not later, when he got into a silly dispute with the City Council and Mayor over when he would retire. When the street cops denied Gates, when they no longer had confidence in his support, he was through.[4]

Over Gates's 14-year tenure as leader, he and the LAPD had espoused a position that, in times of publicized questioning of his officers or his department, amounted to the following:

- We're never wrong.
- It's the other guy's fault.
- It's not our fault.
- It's never our fault.
- We're in the job of keeping the peace and if you don't like it, that's too bad.
- We're not out here to be popular, we're out there to do our job.
- If you're not with us, you're against us.

And since the frontline police supervisors and rank-and-file officers work for the brass, they, too, adopted that position and applied it to their work in the field. If you don't believe this, witness the department's mishandling of the Rodney King riots, in which over $800 million dollars in property was damaged and 52 innocent lives lost. During the vacuum that was LAPD leadership and command during the riots, there was much wringing of hands but little activity. "Contingency plans, what contingency plans?" seems to have been the message from on high.

For a city of that size, which supposedly has an office of disaster preparedness and an emergency operations center inside the police department, where was the tactical action plan that said in bold red letters, "This is how our police department will respond in the event of a major civil disturbance"? The objectives (as they should have been planned, discussed, and trained for in advance) should have been these:

- Maintain order.
- Maintain discipline inside the police department and out on the streets.
- Protect the public.
- Protect the public interest.
- Protect property.

- Serve the city in a variety of ways besides just law enforcement.

Instead, not one drop of tear gas was fired upon any looters, few were arrested for stealing—even though many officers caught them in the act—and, for the most part, LA's finest stood by passively waiting for orders to move out. Those orders, when they finally did arrive, were too late to make much of a difference. By the time the California National Guard came in to shore up the police, most of South Central Los Angeles had been broken or burned.

If you're not ready for a crisis when it comes, then by definition, you will be behind the action curve. You will spend your time reacting to events, rather than proactively managing them. If you don't know your organization's position, core issues, message, and objectives, you will be steamrolled by the activities around you.

What Gates and the LAPD never learned until it was too late was this: if the Cable News Network (CNN) shows a videotape relating to your organization at the top and bottom of every hour for several weeks, you had better have more than a hasty or, worse, off-the-cuff response at the ready.

The CEO as Spokesperson: Make the Message Match the Messenger

In the wake of apparent gross misconduct by an organization that strikes at the core and the heart of what it stands for, the right person to talk is the man or woman in charge. This is the person who can affect change and who can take responsibility. But in the case of the LAPD, what Gates said wasn't right, the way he felt obviously wasn't right, and it's not just who was speaking, but what his message was.

If the leader is so opposed to the message, then it's not that they had the wrong level of person speaking, it's that they had an organizational problem. The whole LAPD issue demonstrated a central organizational problem. It wasn't where it needed to be in terms of its mentality.

Gates should have stood up and said, "I've seen this tape and I'm as horrified as anybody. I'm not going to rush to condemn the officers involved. But we're not going to stop until we know what the facts were and we're going to be very public in that process. And if any of my officers have conducted themselves in a bad way, and frankly, at this point I have some serious questions about their behavior, they will be punished."

This should have qualified as Gates's initial statement, to be followed by well-thought-out subsequent ones as he and his top management gathered more information about the event in question. It's what the various publics want and it's what any good organization should provide in times of crisis.

In events like the Rodney King arrest, an oil spill, a passenger train derailment, an airline crash that kills all aboard, a tainted or otherwise sabotaged product that injures customers, the public sentiment that always comes to bear against companies is this:

> We don't want to hear excuses. We want to know you feel as badly about what happened as we do. We want to know your plans for the immediate future and then for the long term. We don't want to see finger-pointing, stonewalling, or blame being passed around like so much stale bread. We want to hear you talk about your feelings first, your plans second, and the results of those plans and all your other efforts after that.

It's likely that Daryl Gates's strong personality and his "my way or the highway" management style would not have allowed for much compromise or any assumption of blame on his part. It just wasn't his way to say:

> You know, after looking at this tape, I'd like to go on record as saying we need to take an immediate and hard look at the way we do our business. There's going to have to be some changes around here and I'm going to personally start the review process immediately to see what we need to fix to ensure that this kind of incident never happens again.

From a positive public relations standpoint, here are some ideas on preventing a CEO response similar to the misguided efforts applied by Chief Gates.

The CEO needs to be trained in what to say to the media and the other publics during and after a crisis event. This means don't expect your leader (or yourself, if you're the CEO) to be able to stride to the lectern, address a group of hungry newshounds, and wing it. This is no place for a poorly thought-out, unprepared response. Even reading a canned statement is better than attempting to bull your way through a press event that's bound to involve tough questions which you may not be ready or able to answer.

- Know what your message should say in advance.
- Know how to deliver this message to your audience.
- Deliver this message forcefully.
- Stick to your message, but adapt it as necessary.

There are those times when the CEO is *not* the best spokesman for the company. And this is not because he doesn't agree with the message, but because he can't hold his temper. He might not be able to speak adequately or comfortably on camera. Or perhaps, when he does talk on camera, he looks as if he's lying even when he's telling the truth. In such cases, he's just not the right choice.

Keep in mind that, just as there are various levels of management in an organization, there are various response levels as well. It's important not to have the president of the company speak about something that's a divisional problem, because it suddenly elevates the problem. But if it *is* a corporate or organizational problem, you need to have the person in charge do the speaking about it.

> It's always easier to go up to the top instead of go down from the top. If, during the early stages of a problem, you start out with a senior vice president as the spokesperson, it makes sense to escalate up the chain of command and bring in the CEO to clarify matters and redefine the company's position.

When the CEO follows one of his senior people, he can help reposition the company's core message by putting his own mark on it. In many cases, this can serve to help the organization's goodwill with its audiences, educate and reeducate both the media and the public, reduce the potential for future litigation, and, put simply, comfort people inside and outside the organization by his mere presence on scene.

The people who make up your various publics want to see leadership in action and want someone to take ownership of the problem and the solutions. Who these solutions come from can have a huge impact upon their perception of how well or not these events are handled.

Should the CEO start out as the figurehead and then later defer to a vice president or other less-senior-person in the company, the unspoken message about who is really in charge can get muddied.

Messages From On High

If you have a corporate problem or a public relations problem, people want to see that the person in charge is not just the figurehead, but the spokesperson. Chet Burchett comments:

> This is why people hate it when PR people come out on camera and talk. They think, "Here comes the mouthpiece or the hired gun." People also think that what the PR person says about the company doesn't really matter. The PR message gets lost because he or she cannot affect change and is not in charge. The CEO should speak for the company and not allow hired hands to do it. It doesn't mean as much if the CEO is not there. People want to see accountability, responsibility, and they want to understand truth.[5]

Lee Iacocca, when he was the flamboyant head of Chrysler, seemed to have started the trend in advertising that has the head of the firm speak about the products. TV viewers associated him with Chrysler's robust new attitude about building quality cars, and when the minivan revolution hit, he was already in place as the spokesperson for his firm's best-selling line.

And with the fame and glory came the exposure to the heat. While some critics have questioned Iacocca's management style as autocratic and self-centered, there was no question of his fervor, in good times and in bad, and for the health and viability of his company and its employees. He was there to take the hard questions when Chrysler was roiling in a sea of debt and near-insolvency, and he was there when the customer service awards were handed out and the firm was back on its feet.

And today, a number of chief executives have made a new name for themselves via the TV screen. They include: the late Orville Redenbacher of popcorn fame; Dave Thomas from Wendy's; Carl Karcher, chairman emeritus of Carl's Jr.; Victor Kiam, CEO, Remington; Herb Kelleher, CEO, Southwest Airlines; and a number of small and large business owners and founders who have been profiled in an ongoing series of American Express ads.

The point about these CEOs' newly discovered media popularity is not just that it's fun to be famous, but that there can be value and *strength* in this exposure. If a significant crisis struck one of the above firms and the CEO, who has already established himself as a TV celebrity, takes to the lectern, public credibility will be almost instantaneous.

Media Rules to Live or Die By

The following list of positive public relations do's and don'ts should speak for themselves. Ignore them at your peril:

- Don't lie.
- Don't panic.
- Don't lose control.
- Don't get defensive with the media, the public, your customers, or your employees.

- Don't stonewall the media, the public, your customers, or your employees.
- Don't make promises you can't or won't keep.
- Don't put the wrong spokesperson into the wrong role.
- Don't believe anything is ever "off the record" with the press.
- Don't think you have to make a comment about everything.
- Don't let a day pass without correcting a gross media or public relations error.
- Don't think you have to solve everything in one day.
- Above all, be flexible.

Being in front of TV cameras or on the spot with print reporters who have sharpened pencils and sharper tongues at the ready can have even well-trained people feeling like frogs in a glass jar surrounded by scalpel-wielding biology students. This can create a thought process that starts with, "They're all looking at me for answers, so I'd better give them something good or they won't like me, won't think I'm a credible leader, or will write or say something bad about my company."

This desire to speak and justify your existence in the company and your presence in front of the media is both admirable and exceedingly dangerous. You can start by answering one little, seemingly harmless question, and end up saying many things you'll regret later.

Sometimes the CEO's or business owners who speak for everyone in the company can be their own worst enemies. The solution is clear: only speak for your company if you've been trained to do so effectively. If not, hire a qualified PR firm or, barring that because of time or expense, find a well-qualified person in your organization to fill the spokesperson role immediately.

And if you do need to choose someone from inside, be aware that he or she will need some combination of the following traits and skills:

- Some prior experience dealing with the print and TV media, including some in-place sources, contacts, or other professional media relationships who may help out if necessary

- Some hands-on video training (i.e., on-camera experience, gained either in past events or seminar- or consultant-run training; in other words, the person is neither camera-shy nor frozen like a deer caught in headlights)
- Good written communication skills (i.e., he or she can write effective statements, press releases, and other essential company messages on demand)
- Good verbal communications skills (i.e., he or she can give presentations to different audiences and handle the stress of doing so with a certain aplomb)
- A strong sense of professionalism (i.e. he or she remains unflappable during times when most people are flappable)
- Good camera presence (i.e., he or she is reasonably attractive, well-spoken, appropriately attired; in other words, the person can act, dress, and speak the part he or she is supposed to be playing)
- The ability to answer and bridge tough questions (i.e., he or she can keep the company out of legal hot water and still appease the press and the public with accurate answers that support and defend the company's position)
- Knowledge of the company's message, core values, and goals, before, during, and after any significant event and an understanding of the big picture and the long-term ramifications of his or her actions and those of the organization

People have come to expect polished, professional, credible, and even slightly glib spokespeople. Why? Some experts suggest that this expectation comes from our constant exposure to television as the medium for nearly all our messages.

> We look to TV for news, information, and even answers to the troubling questions in our lives. Thanks to the way electronic and video technology has continued to improve by leaps and bounds, people intuitively assume that the *way* this message comes across is almost as important as the message itself.

And so it goes in your company's dealings with the public and the media. There is less room for error or a lack of solid professionalism, than ever before. Most folks have seen thousands of examples of the way things are supposed to be done on TV, and they will come to your situation expecting the same.

Public Relations Recovery Through Service Recovery

There is a way to fix many public relations foul-ups immediately, accurately, and relatively painlessly. It serves as a viable method to keep even the most unreasonable of your publics relatively happy. It's a concept known as *service recovery* and it can really create a noticeable difference between you and your competitors.

Service recovery starts by saying, "We're sorry about what happened and we're going to work hard to make it right." And it helps to let people know that the person in charge of this firm *can* make it right. Put simply, service recovery is exactly what it sounds like: recovering a failed service moment of truth with the use of two simple words: "I'm sorry."

Nothing irritates a customer more than being treated to poor service, for whatever reason, and then not hearing those fateful words from any service employee in the vicinity. Service recovery is really that basic—you or your people should apologize when the situation warrants it. It's amazing how far the phrases, "I'm sorry we made a mistake," "We apologize for any inconvenience we've caused you," or the best answer, "I'm sorry this happened. What can *I* do to correct the problem?" will go to regain customer goodwill.

The moments following a service screwup of any magnitude are critical to your customers. What you do right then *for* them means a lot *to* them. Your fervent activities to correct their problems play a large part in their decision to return and do business with you again. Now is not the time for rationalizations ("We couldn't help it"), excuses ("It was somebody else's fault"), or apathy ("Sorry, that's not my problem, department, or mistake").

Your publics want and need you to help the both of you recover skillfully and gracefully. When you do this well, you win friends. When you don't do it well or at all, you make enemies.

[There's no question, however, that in these days of the never-ending civil suit, your public position should be carefully couched inside your legal position as well.]

You need to exhibit judicious good sense and humanity. You need to understand that you cannot possibly account for every legal extremity. When a serious problem arises, your company is not necessarily guilty of some corporate crime, but you do feel bad about it. That's a big difference. And more important, that's what people want to hear initially.

Of course, following any crisis, most good attorneys worth their salt will say, "You can't just go around saying you're sorry, or they'll get all your money if and when we go to court." That's wrong. Of course, you *should* be sorry about a serious business event that involves lives and property or the health and safety of your employees, customers, or other consumers.

This "Don't apologize, don't admit, don't tell" position is both understandable and historical. Corporate lawyers are paid good money to keep their clients out of court and in cash. It is their collective belief that you should not admit to anything now that might cost you money later. A sign on a veteran attorney's desk says it best:

ADMIT NOTHING
DENY EVERYTHING
DEMAND PROOF

While this defense is admirable, it's also out of step with reality today. As we have seen in other examples throughout this book, the need to speak early and accurately to the various publics involved in any problem related to your business is a key to your success. We will speak to this issue of lawsuit protection in the next chapter, but at this point, try to keep this maxim in mind:

[Saying "we're sorry" is not an admission of guilt.]

They Don't Have to Love You or Even Like You: Earning Respect Through Honesty

The late Malcolm S. Forbes once said, "The only sin in business is not making a profit." While this is arguable on many levels, it brings up a point. The ultimate goal and purpose of your company should be to keep the doors open and the business going. This is not to say that you should continue selling tainted products, step over dead bodies in a workplace violence homicide, or otherwise appear insensitive, insincere, or inhumane. But on the other hand, not everyone has to love you for you to continue to do business. If your firm is publicly held, you have a responsibility to your shareholders, your employees, and your board of directors to carry on, even in the face of a significant crisis.

In the periods during or just after a crisis, some company leaders confuse the need to be loved by all with the desire to be respected by most. It's an important distinction and one that is always easier to express than achieve. Depending upon the nature of the problem, people outside the company don't want to hear that your crisis came about as an act of God, Mother Nature, your vendors, your competitors, or some other group other than you. People want to hear that you're as horrified, disturbed, or worried as any normal human being would be and that you're not going to rest until everything is put right.

Since you can't *please* everyone, instead of trying to make all of the publics happy—a daunting aim in the best of circumstances—focus your efforts on *satisfying* most of your publics.

This doesn't mean that everyone who hears about you, does business with you, or otherwise comes into contact you will leave with a smile, only that you'll know you've done the best you could under trying circumstances. As you think back over the cases of the product, image, and employee problems described in this book (as well as ponder your own experiences) you'll see why certain executive responses achieved the objective of holding or regaining the company's market share after a crisis, while others failed miserably, managing to lose the company's market share or in dire cases, never regain it at all.

Notes

1. *Los Angeles Times,* March 20, 1991.
2. Koon, Sgt. Stacey, with Robert Deitz, *Presumed Guilty,* Washington, D.C.: Regnery Gateway, 1992, p. 109. Copyright © 1992 by Regnery Publishing, Inc. All rights reserved. Reprinted by special permission of Regnery Publishing, Inc., Washington, D.C.
3. Ibid., p. 109.
4. Ibid., p. 109.
5. In-person interview with Chet Burchett, November 18, 1994, Chicago, Illinois.

9

Lawsuits and Sharkskin Suits

How to Keep the Plaintiff and Class-Action Attorneys at Bay

Torts are lawyers' "happy hours"
Like double gin and fizz;
Spelled backward tort is trot,
Straight to the bank, that is.

—Art Buck

Let's get straight to the point: if you own or operate a business today, expect to get sued. It may happen tomorrow or it might happen in 10 years, but it's coming. We live and work in the most litigious society on the planet. There are more attorneys per person in the United States than in any other country in the world. The fact is, if you have employees, products, and services in any combination, chances are good you will be sued by a participant in this Age of Entitled Disgruntlement.

Even in the best of circumstances, if you take all the necessary precautions, you'll still be hit with angry letters from angry attorneys representing angry clients who will *threaten* to sue you. One weary business executive says, "Only in America can the consumer assume almost zero responsibility for his own actions."

Worse yet, thanks to the way some people don't pay your bills, default on your contracts with them, or otherwise renege on their deals with you, you can expect to find your company in court as a plaintiff as well. The point of all this is clear: you stand a good chance of ending up in court in some fashion or form if you engage in commerce. Business guru Tom Peters puts it this way:

> American society suffers from a debilitating disease at exactly the wrong time: an urgent desire to be protected from all risks. At the drop of a hat someone will sue his or her broker for lousy stock picks or a manufacturer for designing a ladder that doesn't perform well when both legs are placed on ice.[1]

Perhaps this explains how or why a woman sued United Airlines in October 1994 for $5 million after baggage handlers accidently loaded her poodle on a plane headed for Nebraska instead of Los Angeles. Or why, in May 1994, Remington Arms had to pay $17 million to a Texas deer hunter who shot himself in the foot with one of their rifles. *Forbes* reporter Robert J. Samuelson echoes this "run to a lawyer" phenomenon:

> America does not have too many lawyers because the pay is too high. Rather, we have too many lawyers because Americans try to deal with every problem or complaint with a new law, regulation, or lawsuit.[2]

That's the bad news—that there are lots of lawyers out there and that you can expect to be sued for some real or imagined wrong by some person or group of people who see your firm as having lots of insurance, deep pockets, or both.

The good news is that that's why you have insurance and that's why you pay those premiums, consult with your own in-house or outside attorneys, and think in terms of risk management and liability protection. To put it simply, getting sued today should be seen as a cost of doing business in the 1990s and beyond. So why spend your days and nights worrying about every deal coming undone or about lone plaintiffs lurking in the shadows? Accept the realities of litigation in business today and arm yourself and your company accordingly.

A View From the Law Office and the Courtroom

Much of what follows is drawn from the legal wisdom of attorney Stephen Fitch, senior partner of the San Diego, California, law firm Fitch & Associates. Unless otherwise noted, the quoted passages are taken from an exclusive interview with Fitch in San Diego on January 15, 1995. His practice is mainly in civil litigation, tax, and corporate law, but he also specializes in representing government agencies, planning boards, fire districts, and other business and legislative groups that often become embroiled in crisis-related events. These associations require attorney services to keep them lawsuit-free and out of legal, liability, or risk-based entanglements.

Keep in mind that some of the things espoused by Chet Burchett (see Chapters 7 and 8) will not be the same as those advised by Steve Fitch. Attorneys and PR people have different agendas based upon the needs of their particular clients. And their training, backgrounds, and experiences can often call for them to answer the same question in completely different ways.

What all this means is that, while each man has his opinions about the best way to respond to an organizational crisis related to products, image, or employees, or how to deal with media or public relations issues, or how to handle the threat or occurrence of civil suits, one size should not fit all. Your business is not their business, your customers or clients are not theirs, and your problems may be completely unique to your company or your industry. Balance what each of these professionals says with your own good judgment and your particular business needs.

Forewarned Is Forearmed: A Yearly Review With Your Attorney

Small-to-midsize business owners, because of the nature of their organizations, usually don't have access or even the need for large law firms, in-house corporate counsel, or a specific place on-site known as the Legal Department. Because this is so, they need to establish a relationship with an outside attorney to help them steer clear of potential problem areas over the short- and long-term.

Most lawyers will charge anywhere from $100 to $200 per hour to review your business practices and procedures with an eye toward your liability risks. Steve Fitch says, "It's worth your time to spend one or two hours once or twice per year just going to your attorney's office and talking about what you are doing in your business."

Any company with five or more employees particularly needs this service. Most take it, but some business people are either lawyer-aversive (because they have had one or more bad experiences with attorneys), too frugal to see the wisdom of buying attorney consultation time, or too stubborn to realize that unless they have a juris doctorate themselves, they will need expert legal advice at some time in the near future.

By laying the groundwork for this kind of relationship, you not only get expert legal advice with regard to any liability issues, but, during problem periods, already have an ally in your corner. Says Fitch:

> Should you find yourself in a crisis situation, and you call the attorney for advice, you don't have to waste time and money acquainting him or her with you or the nature of your business. It becomes easier for the attorney to step into an assistance mode if he or she knows more about who you are and what you do.

> Searching through the phone book for legal help in a crisis is like looking for a roofer in a rainstorm. Not only is it difficult to think clearly or choose proper counsel in the midst of a crisis, it also forces you to trust a stranger with what could be the lifeblood of your company should you have to quickly bring him or her on board.

If you already have a preestablished relationship with a law firm whom you trust and find dependable, you'll be in much better shape than if you have to bring one into your company at a time when people are racing through the halls pulling out their hair and screaming.

What's worse, says Fitch, is when company leaders or executives expect a new attorney to come on the scene and immediately save the day following the onset of a serious problem. Without the proper background, knowledge of the business and its practices and problems, it only makes a hard situation for the attorney even tougher. Even the most basic or rudimentary information given in advance can help the attorney make the right decision later and under pressure. He comments on this practice of bringing lawyers into the fold at the last minute:

> I get calls from companies who are in the middle of situations and want me to step in and solve the problems. I'm often reluctant because, like them, I'm a businessperson too and I have to worry about my goodwill and reputation in the community. Before I say that we'll help them, I want to find out more about the people calling me, the type of business they have, are they the kind of client I want to or can represent, and if there is a conflict with other clients.

In keeping with this idea of being forewarned, Fitch suggests that you schedule at least an annual assessment of your liability issues with your attorney. He says, "As part of your year-end review that you always do as a businessperson in December or January, schedule time with your attorney to review the past year and look toward the next one."

Your Liability Review: Enough Insurance? An Action Plan?

To make a sweeping generalization (which also happens to be absolutely true) there are two ways to protect your business during potentially serious situations: (1) have enough and the right kind of insurance; and (2) do the right thing. While this book has addressed the latter, your attorney is also keenly interested in the former, largely because the world of insurance—assumed risk, injury or damage claims, liability issues, and hard dollars—falls into your lawyer's domain as often as it does your insurance agent's, if not more so. Good attorneys will have copies of your insurance policies on hand and will at the least be familiar with the language and coverages for each.

Fitch warns, however, that insurance is not a totally saving grace:

> Something that is a peril to a person or to property is generally covered by insurance. The problem with insurance is that simply to say, "I'm covered by insurance, so I've protected myself" isn't necessarily true. In the long term, this view can be extremely shortsighted.

[It's important to know what your business insurance *will* cover and what no amount of insurance will ever *recover.*]

Will your liability insurance protect your direct bottom line following a significant, expensive event? Will your insurance pay for your attorneys' fees, losses, monetary damage claims, and other associated expenses should you need to close, move, or replace your assets? Usually, the answer is yes to both questions. But what about your company's good name, its goodwill, its established public confidence, the way customers and consumers have relied on the integrity and honesty of your products and services in the past? Who pays the hidden costs when those valuable commodities go down the drain following a significant problem?

Can you become involved in a episode costing hundreds, thousands, or millions of dollars and not lose a penny from your bottom line? "Yes," argue insurance brokers, insurance salespeople, and their representative firms, "that's what you have us and our policies for." But can you go and buy back customer loyalty? Can you snap your fingers and make your customers believe that your products and services are safe, viable, and worthy again? Where is the insurance policy for lost business, as when herds of customers head past your business in search of your competitors' doorways? Says Steve Fitch:

> Do you have to have insurance? That's a good question to ask. I say yes. Any business owner or operator

> should have at least a basic level of insurance coverage. It's the sheet on the bottom of the bed, before you start putting the blankets on top to protect you. You must have other layers besides insurance. Understand this: no matter what business you run, from a small retail firm to a large conglomerate, you will, at some time during your business life, suffer a crisis. Insurance only offers one level of the protection you need and require.

He continues along this line, discussing the need for companies and their people to plan for problems:

> You have a choice in business: you can either be proactive or reactive to crises. The way you prepare, from a legal standpoint, is to look first at your insurance coverage, then decide if you have addressed any potential legal concerns with your attorney in your plant, office, store, or business, and finally, have a plan if a problem arrives you cannot handle. Do you know where to seek help and resources right away?

Employees as Plaintiffs: Labor Law Problems

Your initial or ongoing liability reviews with your attorney should focus on what you both see as your biggest areas of concern in terms of risk. It may be the products you make, the presence of potentially hazardous substances you create or use to make those products, the types of work your employees do, transportation issues, or, in this era of the debate between employment at will versus the right to work, employee problems.

Attorney Fitch sees this last area as one of the most difficult and business threatening for the years to come.

> Most business owners are poorly equipped to deal with employee-related problems. Most of them have the mindset that says, "We've never had a problem before now, so we're never going to have a problem."

> However, how you treated your employees fifteen, ten, or even five years ago may not have resulted in liability back then because they weren't considered actionable. Today, employee treatment is an area filled with huge civil suits. Five years ago, an employee mistreated at work might have said, "I need this job so I'll just put up with it." Now, they say, "I can leave this job and make lots and lots of money by suing."

Peter C. Robertson, from the Organizational Resources Counselors, says, "In the current environment, no company is immune from these lawsuits."[3]

Steve Fitch still sees business owners and executives who say, with regard to employee problems, "This is my business. I'll run it the way I want." To fall back on the premise that insurance will protect you is extremely shortsighted. Don't think insurance will serve as your security blanket for every liability issue, warns Fitch:

> There's no insurance for most employee-related problems. If your liability insurance carrier ever denies you coverage for areas outside your policy, you're suddenly faced with a claim in which you'll have to use your resources, cash flow, and assets to pay an attorney to defend you. You can imagine this is not a good position to be in. You could find yourself having your business destroyed or lost simply because you didn't understand what the current climate is concerning how you treat your employees.

The frightening part is that if you're in charge and you allow certain conditions to flourish—sexual harassment, workplace violence, drug or alcohol abuse that causes stress claims or injury, or dangerous working conditions not covered by safety devices, training, or instructions—you can become an automatic party to any litigation, even if you were not directly involved. If the plaintiff's attorney can argue that you knew Mary Jones was being harassed by your manager, Bill Smith, and yet you did nothing to intervene, your name may appear on the lawsuit along with Bill's.

The rules about employee treatment have been around for years. Now, thanks to heightened awareness, these rules are getting enforced by the federal government, by attorneys, and by plaintiff-employees who say, "That was then and this is now. I will no longer suffer mistreatment at my workplace."

"If all you focus on with your employees," says Steve Fitch, "is their 9-to-5 matters, you're setting yourself up for some real problems in the future. These days, and in this labor relations environment, employers have to function almost like a parental figure."

With the prevalence of off-the-job problems, it's just no longer possible to tell your employees to check their troubles and their emotions at the door. In some cases, managers who don't have their finger on the pulse of the organization will not be able to react to employee problems that affect the workplace until they are well past the point of repair. Allowing employees with behavior difficulties to work unchecked shouldn't happen without intervention.

The Need for Ongoing Training

In this day and time, there is absolutely no excuse for not being aware, trained, and informed about the latest employee-related laws, labor practices, Occupational Safety and Health Act (OSHA) rules, employment standards, and hiring requirements. In every major city, you can find consultants, seminar leaders, and other experts to teach in-house programs for your firm and its executives, managers, and supervisors. There are highly specific seminars on sexual harassment training; workplace violence prevention; ADA (Americans with Disabilities Act) rules and regulations; AIDS awareness; legal hiring and prescreening procedures; new discipline and termination practices; drug and alcohol abuse on the job; employee assistance programs; and legal issues relating to labor unions, etc.

Take advantage of all the ongoing employee-related and employee management training you can attend, bring in, or schedule for your department heads. Ignorance of the law is no longer a viable defense in court. Your insurance rates, coverages, and payouts may depend on how much you know about not just your business, but your employee practices as well.

If you're in charge, give your training department an immediate mandate to give you an operational HRD training plan. It doesn't have to be wall-to-wall from the start, but it had better include provisions for hiring and supervision training or retraining every manager and supervisor at the different levels of your organization.

It may help to look at training as an investment in the future. In times of tight money, when managers are constantly being asked to do more with less, training is one of the first sacrificial lambs in the budget. Training must be seen as basic a cost of doing business, not an added expense. Any investment you can make in worthwhile, legitimate training programs that provide your firm with more information than it had originally, is worth the price.

The Best Defense Is a Strong Offense: Staying Clear of the Courtroom

For many people in business, there are few more chilling documents than a Notice to Appear In Court. Even if you're not named specifically, the fact that your company's name is attached to a piece of paper that says "You Are Being Sued" can strike fear in even the most stout corporate hearts.

But there is a paradox at work here. Just because you or your legal counsel (in-house or outside attorney) receives an official-looking form requiring a court appearance should not be cause for immediate alarm. After all, as this chapter has pointed out, anyone can sue anyone for anything. Civil papers are not like the Hope diamond. If you can get to the courthouse and file the paperwork, you could sue Mother Teresa if you so desired.

But what prevents most people or companies from suing you in borderline cases is the possibility that they could get socked with your legal fees as well as theirs. Steve Fitch explains:

In the majority of business transactions, there is an attorney's fees provision in the agreement. This requires both sides and their legal counsel to think very hard before they step in and file a lawsuit against the other party, because there is a risk they'll have to pay attorneys' fees if they're wrong. So they have to think consciously about it and make a prudent decision first. It's not the same with the average citizen. Tort reform will force people to think twice before filing a lawsuit based on shaky grounds. Lawsuits are filed today simply because some people know it will cause an expense to an insurance company, who will offer some money, which is less than the company would pay to litigate the matter.

To Settle or Not to Settle: Avoiding the Michael Jackson Syndrome

One of the problems with both legitimate and nuisance lawsuits is the relationship to that old bugaboo known as the sunk-cost theory. Whether you call it "throwing good money after bad" or "spending a dollar to save a dime," the results are the same. In many sunk-cost deals, companies and their leaders get caught up in the idea that if they just continue to ride out the storm, and after some unspecified amount of time, things will get suddenly better. If you had unlimited resources and all the money in the world to throw at these problems, perhaps this would be true. Since most firms have little of either to spare, they need to decide when it's financially, legally, ethically, and morally appropriate to cut their losses and move on.

> Sometimes it *is* cheaper and more effective to settle a court suit and get the whole matter off your hands.

In cases where your liability is crystal clear, what is the point of hashing out the whole mess in costly and time-intensive litigation? Would you rather spend $100,000 in legal fees and still not guarantee vindication in court, or settle the case for $10,000 and get back to business?

This is, of course, a simplistic solution to what might be a very difficult problem, but the point should be clear: your decision to settle any pending litigation should be based on extensive meetings with your attorney and your own review of what constitutes the best use of your firm's time and money.

All of this leads us to the biggest caveat of all when it comes to out of court settlements: the perception of guilt, wrongdoing, or other malfeasance by the various publics who witness the events firsthand, or more commonly, secondhand, through the media.

Few recent cases have brought this perception to light more sharply than pop singer Michael Jackson's apparent settlement with the minor who alleged that he sexually molested him. The initial news of Jackson's suggested involvement in this kind of criminal behavior caused many of his fans to question their faith in him. And since his life was already viewed as more than a bit eccentric anyway, even his strongest supporters found themselves in the awkward position of asking, "Could it be true?"

While the media storm cascaded around Jackson, the case split in the public along the lines of those who believed the allegations, those who didn't, and some who just didn't know, but if pressed, would say that they sided with the child and his family. But as Mary A. Fischer put it in her article on Jackson:

> It is, of course, impossible to prove a negative—that is, prove that something *didn't* happen. Given the slim evidence against Jackson, it seems unlikely he would have been found guilty had the case gone to trial. But in the court of public opinion, there are no restrictions. People are free to speculate as they wish, and Jackson's eccentricity leaves him vulnerable to the likelihood that the public has assumed the worst about him.[4]

The simple fact is that most of the public believes that if you settle a court case you must be guilty. Why? Because thanks to many other high-profile civil cases that have been settled before the court date with "undisclosed amounts" and "no admission of wrongdoing" by the party with the open checkbook, most of us conclude, quite logically, that the losing/paying side wouldn't have settled if they thought they could have won the case.

Hence, the Michael Jackson syndrome kicks in for many firms who, even if they are right, merely wish to rid themselves of costly litigation. Could they have proved their innocence in court? Probably. And will settling the case help them or hurt them as they try to get back to business? This could depend on whether they are a large, publicly recognized company with well-known products or services, or a smaller, less visible organization.

Will the company throw good money down the attorney's fees drain in the process if it fights? In most cases, yes. Is it easier for it to pay a small settlement and leave now or wait and risk paying big later? That's a question only careful thought and a hard look into the future can answer.

So this leads to several tough decisions: Do we fight or settle? Do we risk bad publicity now and hope the public will forget about this incident in the months and years to come? Or do we pour all of our dollars, energies, and resources into fighting for our good name? Is it more important for us to win in the court of public opinion now or later? Do we want to wait to prevail in court one, two, or five years from today or should we take our lumps now and move on?

Without the answers to these and other questions, you can't proceed with much confidence. Emotions (i.e., "Screw those people! Let's fight it out!") should not be your guiding force. Your involvement in a court case should start and remain as a good "dollars-and-sense" decision, not one based on who is bigger or smarter. Wisdom based on experience, intelligent suggestions from your legal counsel, and plain common sense should be your ongoing guide.

All that having been said, when *should* you consider settling, and when should you fight it out in court? In many cases, it might not even be your decision. Today, we have insurance policies and claims adjusters who are paid to make that decision for you. Your involvement in many legal issues requiring the presence of your insurance people may take you out of the decision-making process completely. Their role—and what you pay their premiums for—is to gather all the facts from you, collect as much information as they can from the other side, speak to counsel from both sides, and then make a decision, which, in a seemingly high majority of cases, is to settle the case and move on.

In still other cases where your insurance company does not become involved, *you* may choose to settle a case to protect your goodwill and to keep your customers happy. This is common in many small-claims-court suits or other instances where the dollar figures either don't justify involving your insurance company or you feel you have the resources to handle them in-house.

Further, if you're in a high-liability position, it may be best to settle the case early. There is little value to reminding your publics about the case every time something happens with it. It may be of more value for you to suffer through two or three weeks of hard and public legal times with the hope that within six months, it's forgotten. While such forgetfulness is less likely after high-profile cases involving significant losses, injuries, or deaths, it may be possible to ride out the bad press, take some shots to the chin, and go on in many other instances.

If you asked company executives and their lawyers whether they would choose low-liability cases with major public relations problems versus high-liability cases with minor public relations problems, most would choose to deal with the former.

You probably can ride out most bad public relations problems using some of the methods described in this book—especially since it's cheaper to use positive public relations and effective media management techniques instead of paying out high settlement costs. Liability dollars can pour out of your coffers (or via your insurance company) in buckets. If you have a choice, take the low liability and roll the public relations dice.

Heading to Court: The Value of Your Good Name

Sometimes you just have to say to all who will listen, including your attorneys, who may be advising settlement, "It's important for us to protect our company and our company name. We're right, we know it, and more important, we can prove it in court."

Recent history has demonstrated this in courthouses throughout the land; companies have said to suing plaintiffs, "We believe in the strength of our position. We refuse to settle, and we will have our day in court." It's hard to put a dollar value on the need to protect your good name and reputation. While it may be cheaper to settle, sometimes going to court should be more than just an economic decision. Sometimes it is simply the right thing to do over the long term and for the message you want to send to people who view your results.

Knowing you're right and later proving it in court can have a dramatic impact upon your future business success. "For one thing," says attorney Steve Fitch, "it sends a strong message to any 'sharks' out there who think your company is an easy target that will roll over and settle any nuisance suit."

If your firm is perceived as being a tough litigator that fights when it's right, you may be able to avoid this kind of suit by taking a strong early stand. For the fence-sitter plaintiffs out there—those people or groups who may be waiting for a chance to press their agenda against your company—knowing that you will go to the mat with them every time may send them looking for other targets.

With every legal question or dilemma, it's always easy to look at things in the light of hindsight. This book does that in quantities, mostly because it's hard to *predict* when and where bad things will happen. We may be able to identify some of the warning signs and symptoms for problem people, problem products, and the potential for image disasters, but as our litigation-filled courts continue to demonstrate, no one or no company is completely bullet-proof.

If you have had some kind of operational failure, admit it and don't look to place the blame elsewhere. You will better prevail in the public venue if you are perceived as candid, responsive, and honest. The companies who get hammered in the courtroom are those who seek to hide their flaws until the truth reveals them.

Notes

1. Peters, Tom, "Emphasize the Right Stuff," *Forbes* ASAP, February 27, 1995, p. 110.
2. "Other Comments," *Forbes,* May 8, 1995, p. 30.
3. Mitchell, Russell, "The SWAT Team of Bias Litigation," *BusinessWeek,* January 23, 1995, p. 88.
4. Fischer, Mary A., "Did Michael Do It?," *GQ,* October 1994, p. 214.

10

The Management of Protection

Adding Armor to the Chain of Command and Mortar to the Walls Around You

> The desire for safety stands against every great and noble enterprise.
>
> —Tacitus (130–55 B.C.)

One of the inspirations for this book was a 1993 segment on the CBS news show *60 Minutes.* As I was completing my workplace violence book *Ticking Bombs,* I began to think more and more about how certain people, episodes, and events, such as protesters, trespassers, workplace violence, strikes, boycotts, product or image disasters, could affect the overall health, physical and psychological security, and survivability of a firm. A mere 15 minutes of TV time on a Sunday evening convinced me that most company leaders were not doing enough to protect their organizations and employees from most kinds of harm.

The pivotal *60 Minutes* piece was about a man dying of the AIDS virus who had made it his mission in life to speak out about his disease and urge action and protest among other AIDS supporters. One of his primary targets was the pharmaceutical industry. It was his belief—and one shared by his associates, fellow patients, and supporters—that the prices for AIDS-related drugs were barbarously high and that it was his duty to confront these drug companies in the hope that they would be more philanthropic with their medicines.

Clearly, this form of biomedical debate has many ethical twists and turns. There are those who believe the pharmaceutical manufacturers have every right to charge a high price for their drugs, largely because so much of their money goes into R&D, testing, FDA approval processes, and the marketing of these drugs. They need to charge high prices in order to recoup this initial investment of millions of dollars.

The AIDS patients/rights groups counter that to charge top dollar for a potentially lifesaving drug for now-terminal patients is inhumane and greedy and smacks of corporate insensitivity. To this end, the protesters are willing to do whatever it takes to call attention to their plight. If this means trespassing on the drug companies' property and getting arrested, so be it. Bring on the news cameras and the reporters.

And so it went, as captured by the *60 Minutes* cameras. Here was a group of committed, dedicated, and clearly angry AIDS patients and protesters storming the corporate offices of a drug company and taking over the reception area.

The activists quickly sat on the floor and before linking hands, slipped their arms inside pieces of large-diameter plastic piping. (This is a common tactic used by proponents of civil disobedience; if your hands and wrists are covered by pipe, the police can't easily handcuff you.)

While this scene was unfolding in the foyer, other activists were chaining themselves to the company's front gates, and worse, to the doors and axles of its delivery trucks.

You can imagine the bedlam that erupted during these activities. With news cameras rolling and protesters singing and chanting, several of the drug company's executives ventured into the glare of this newly created limelight. The looks on their faces were just like the ones mountain motorists see as they round a curve at night and catch a surprised deer in their headlights.

To put it simply, here was a public relations crisis of growing proportions, and these company executives had absolutely no idea what to do first, last, or in the middle.

Whether you agree or disagree with these tactics, you must

admit that the event got the attention of the people who worked for the drug company. Their inaction, indecision, and utter panic fueled the pages you are holding. Corporate self-defense also means knowing why, how, and when to protect your inside world from the demands, schemes, and dangers of the outside world.

Advice From a Corporate Security Expert

It's always best to get expert advice in serious matters. And the most serious matters are the protection of your company, its people, its assets, its products, its cash, and its psychological and physical health.

Few people in this country have the experience, background, and expertise of Gavin de Becker, founder of Gavin de Becker Inc., a Los Angeles–based security consulting firm that serves as one of the leading corporate security and threat-assessment centers in this country. Much of the hands-on advice regarding corporate security in this chapter is drawn from an extensive interview with him in Studio City, California, December 14, 1994.

De Becker's Hollywood and *Fortune* 500 client list reads like a virtual who's-who of the famous. His speciality lies in the area of collecting and analyzing threat literature and then developing responses to these threats, which are often aimed at celebrities, politicians, and highly visible business people.

De Becker and his colleagues designed Mosaic-5, a computer-assisted assessment system used for evaluating employees who might act out violently. He designed seminar systems for the U.S. Supreme Court, the Federal Reserve Board, and the U.S. Marshals Service, among others.

De Becker's work in the corporate security arena starts with educating his business clients as to the need to change their perception of the relative safety of the world where we live. Crime and violence and other kinds of disruptive and inappropriate behaviors have come to the workplace. "Generally speaking," he says, "we would all like to think these kinds of problems and events are not part of running a business. Unfortunately, they have become a substantial part of business today."

It's Not Just the Events; It's Fear of the Events

Problems that now occur in the workplace—theft, sabotage, vandalism, violence aimed at co-workers and supervisors, domestic violence victims who are threatened by their partners at work, irrational trespassers, disgruntled customers, and workplace drug and alcohol abuse—all create a climate of fear.

To put it bluntly, says Gavin de Becker:

> Fear is. It exists. There is no "inappropriate" fear. If people feel afraid, they are, for whatever reason. Fear is the capable enemy of productivity and the destroyer of any kind of creative thinking. All employers have to manage fear in the workplace, fear of other co-workers, and the fear of what they might do. It is, at best, a kind of telegram that says there are some questions to ask about these circumstances. There are some things you must do to evaluate the potential for problems.

As you consider the quality of worklife inside your organization, what kinds of situations, if left unchecked, create a climate of fear?

- Can employees and co-workers characterize their fears?
- Are these fears specific?
- Can these fears be characterized in ways that would readily explain why they exist in the first place?

Says de Becker: "Co-workers may have supported fear or unsupported fear. Whichever it is, it is indeed something to be managed."

Whether or not the fears are specific ("I've seen a gun in his lunchbox," as opposed to "He makes me feel uncomfortable whenever he comes around") they are *real* to the people who have them. It's no longer possible (or legal) to wait for these problems to miraculously go away. Gavin de Becker puts it this way:

> Employers must be ready to evaluate these situations. In terms of situations involving workplace violence, I tell employers to do what they would do if you assumed you would be reading about it in *Newsweek*. Every single step you take or fail to take will be the subject of scrutiny later on.

And de Becker echoes a sentiment captured elsewhere in this book, "There are two forms of liability protection," he says, "One is insurance, which is the least significant when compared to the other, which is doing the right thing."

The Myth of "No Past Problems"

Look at the fine print posted at the bottom of every mutual fund prospectus on the market. In four-point type, it says, "Past performance is no guarantee of future results." And so it goes with security issues relating to you and your company. The following statement bears repeating and posting somewhere in a position where you will gaze upon it often:

[Just because nothing has happened in the past is no guarantee that nothing will happen in the future.]

This statement should be the theme for all your future responses, planning, and thinking. Believing anything less than this means you are not in touch with the reality of life outside your own corporate walls.

Flip a coin 100 times and record the results. After 99 flips, heads might come up 99 times. But there is absolutely no guarantee that heads will come up again on the hundredth flip just because it has appeared with such frequency before. And yet this same past history flaw becomes the shaky foundation on which many firms base their security needs, responses, policies, and procedures. This kind of thinking leads to the following kinds of statements:

- "We've never had much of a theft problem around here, so why should we spend the money on new locks?"
- "We've never had a significant workplace violence here before, so why should we worry about one in the future?"
- "Nothing's ever happened in our employee parking lot before. Why put out the added cost for extra security cameras when past history just doesn't warrant it?"
- "All these computer, E-Mail, and voice-mail security devices are tedious and time-consuming. We've never had a problem with fraud or sabotage. It seems a shame to punish our honest workers with too many technical restrictions."
- "We've never had a problem with trespassers, vandals, or protesters in the past. That stuff happens to other companies."

Gavin de Becker puts it this way,

> Everywhere where anything ever happened, nothing had ever happened before. This attitude is fine from a purely statistical standpoint. If you say, "Odds are, nothing will happen here," you may be correct. The issue of foreseeability is what should be applied to your understanding of liability. Is it foreseeable in a factory that employs 10,000 people that one of those employees might cause fear in others? Is it foreseeable that one employee might cause violence to others? Absolutely. No manager or executive can tell me that they are not aware, in today's climate, of the fact

that people do commit multiple shootings in the workplace.

The Environment as Leading Indicator

The need for an ethical, safe, and secure work environment starts at the top and works down. The executives, managers, and supervisors must create an all-pervading sense that says, "We care about what goes on here. It's not just about how many products or services we can sell or make, but more important, what we can do for each other while we accomplish those things."

This is where the company leadership needs to already have in place the rules, regulations, and requirements that make for a better, safer, and healthier workplace. The psychological atmosphere should be so strong that an employee wouldn't even have to think twice about bringing a suspected case of sexual harassment, workplace violence, racial problems, employee theft, embezzlement, product tampering, or any other minor or major problem to the direct attention of any supervisor or manager in the organization.

Where many companies run into trouble is in creating or permitting an atmosphere that discourages rather than encourages people to come forward and express their concern about potential or ongoing problems. This starts with the kind of manager who says, "Don't bring me your personnel (or personal) problems. I'm not interested in that stuff. Just do your work." It exists when employees hear a supervisor say, "Don't be a snitch or a tattletale about every little thing around here. Just stick to your work and keep your nose out of other people's business."

This kind of not-my-problem attitude sends a number of strong and wrong signals to employees, especially to those who work at entry-level or frontline positions. For one, it tells them that management doesn't care much about them or their problems, save those that directly impact their work. It tells the marginal employees that this is a no-consequence workplace where, if you're careful and work hard not to get caught, you can get away with almost anything.

These marginal employees can create tremendous morale problems relating to fear in the workplace. If the marginal employee knows he can steal, damage equipment, threaten, intimidate, or even assault a co-worker without much fear of punishment by the company, what's to stop him?

And what's to stop fence-sitter employees who may have stifled their impulses toward theft, embezzlement, vandalism, or workplace violence until it became clear that management is not tuned to the potential for problems, doesn't appear to care, or is too afraid to intervene? Talk about a case of the inmates running the asylum.

It's this kind of toxic environment that leads to the kinds of cases we read about in the newspaper. At first, a disgruntled employee brings a gun to work and stores it in his locker. Next, he shows it to some co-workers and suggests that he will "take care of anyone who messes with him at work." Then he shows it to his main target of ire and says, "Stay outta my way, or you're next."

Finally, after he has gone over the edge and shot his supposed tormentor, worried managers and executives stand around in small circles wringing their hands and saying, "How could this terrible thing have happened? Why didn't anyone ever come to us before it ever got this bad?"

Following one of these tragedies and under the glare of the media lights, it's not uncommon to hear an employee say, "We tried to tell them," or "Nobody seemed to know what was going on around here." For senior management to act shocked at this late date is shortsighted, and in these litigious times, expensive.

The adage "You reap what you sow" fits perfectly here. At what point did this company allow itself to get so far removed from the needs and concerns of its employees? When did it allow managers and supervisors to *discourage* their people from reporting security problems? At what point did the Security Director and his or her people fail to see the warning signs, stop talking with the employees on a daily basis, or disregard their gut instincts about any employee behavior problem?

There is nowhere to place the blame other than with top management. The senior executives in any company set the ground rules, make the policies, initiate the procedures, and create the psychological environment for the company and its employees.

Think of your own work experiences. If you worked for a very autocratic leader who surrounded himself or herself with like-minded autocratic subordinates, was not the work environment throughout the company also mostly autocratic?

And while the converse may be true (i.e., nurturing managers who empower their employees create a nourishing environment) is it not more difficult to change a toxic work environment into a nourishing one? And is it not easier to start with a nourishing atmosphere and continue to nurture it?

Fear and Toxicity: Why Do We Make It So Wrong to Be Right?

Gavin de Becker tells his corporate clients they need to change their definitions of what is wrong. Too often, companies punish their managers for speaking up, especially in situations where the threat of employee problems, outside problems, or other events or disasters is not immediately imminent.

In such situations, when a manager or a supervisor calls attention to an employee, procedure, event, or any threat to the company's liability, there is an climate that says either, "Handle this yourself; that's why we pay you to be manager in the first place," or "Don't bother us with that right now. Get back to your business."

The problem at hand could be anything from a tainted or defective product to a hazardous condition in the facility, a potentially disgruntled employee who may act out violently to the possibility of an event such as a strike, boycott, or protest that may put the company at some form of significant risk. According to de Becker:

> I suggest to corporate clients that they use new definitions of *wrong*. One would be that you didn't ex-

press your opinion clearly, early, and explicitly. In workplace violence cases, for example, in nearly every case someone comes forward afterwards and says, "I knew this was going to happen," or "I thought he was the kind of guy who would end up doing something like this."

De Becker believes that the problem of management accountability—or, more specifically, of management's *failure* to either recognize or act on employee concerns—stems from this creation of an environment in which employees are encouraged, through various policies or practices (largely unwritten), *not* to report problems or concerns, or *not* to come to top management when their fears reach a certain discomforting level.

De Becker's next definition of *wrong* is when the company or its executives do not put employee, organization, and environmental safety first. When a supervisor comes to his or her boss and says, "One of our workers was exposed to some chemicals," or "One of our machines is not working correctly and may injure someone," or "I think one of my people needs counseling for his drinking problem," and the boss says, "I'll take care of it next week" or "let me be the judge of what our employees need," it's not only wrong, it's *dangerous.*

De Becker's last definition of *wrong* is when the company leaders don't ask the right questions of their employees. This may be a problem on several levels, but usually it is because the people in the key positions—personnel, HRD, EAP, EEO, security—did not train other managers and supervisors to ask the right questions of their reporting employees in the first place.

Clearly, it becomes the duty of the people in the know (department heads and senior executives) to help train other, less-knowledgeable supervisors in how to investigate employee claims and concerns tactfully, legally, ethically, responsively, and, when possible, quickly.

If you or your people do each of these things, says de Becker—express your opinion about a potential problem early and clearly, put employee and company safety first, and ask the right questions before, during, and after any investigation process—you can't be held wrong in what you do. "Unfortunately," he says, "in corporate America, managers and supervisors use the following definitions for wrong" from the point of view of senior management:

- You bothered us.
- You annoyed us.
- You made us nervous without cause.
- You wasted our time.
- You wasted our money.
- Nothing you predicted happened.

[Your managers and supervisors should always feel confident and comfortable coming to senior management with the 5 or 10 percent of the problems they just cannot fix or those few employees whom they just cannot manage.]

If this is not the message your people have in your organization, things need to change.

Changing Your Employees' Reward System

Look hard at the reporting procedures for security problems in your company. Do you encourage your employees to come forward, or are your systems and procedures designed to make them bite their tongues? De Becker says that the latter is common in many companies:

> Employers can take certain steps that have no downside. These things improve life for all employees. Such things as encouraging employees to report potential security problems and establishing a criteria for *what's* reported and *how* it is reported.

There should be no penalties or disincentives for your employees, managers, and supervisors to react, investigate, report, and follow up on company problems. But again, de Becker says, we have the reward system inverted:

> Company leaders need to tell their managers and supervisors, "We do not expect you to make behavioral science assessments. If you can manage the 90 percent of your people with no problems, you're doing unbelievably well. We expect that there will be some number, like 10 percent of people, you won't be able to manage." In fact, what most companies are saying to supervisors is the opposite message: "If you bring us these kinds of problems, it means you're a bad supervisor. Why couldn't you handle it?" All over America there are supervisors who are having to manage situations, and they are understandably reluctant to carry the message upward because they will be viewed as someone who failed as a manager.

It should come as no surprise that this approach does little to inspire a supervisor's confidence in top management's direction or support. Instead of playing "Let's kill the messenger," executives need to say:

> *We relish the opportunity to solve these kinds of problems with you and for you. We will not take a head-in-the-sand approach, no matter how bad it gets. It's your job to bring these problems to us if you cannot solve them alone. We expect and encourage you to seek out the resources at your disposal. We will give you the assistance and guidance you need.*

All employees, no matter what their level, title, or job, should be *encouraged* to report any potential workplace concerns to any one or more of the following:

- Their first-line supervisor
- Any manager
- Any security officer
- The director of security
- Anyone attached to the personnel, human resources, employee assistance, equal employment, or legal departments

And *how* to report workplace problems or concerns is just as important as *whom* to report them to. Company leaders can talk all they want about how they encourage timely reporting, but if they don't give their employees a variety of reporting methods to assist them, it's as bad as not asking in the first place.

The right kind of employee-friendly reporting systems must be in place to help the appropriate people in your organization gather the information, suggestions, or concerns and then act on them. If people are more comfortable making anonymous reports—as happens in small firms or ones where there is much perceived antagonism between worker groups and management—then you'll need to develop some discreet way to collect this data.

Anonymous or not, employees must be able to view the reporting process as being as stress-free as possible. Remember, coming forward to tell a supervisor about a company or employee problem is no easy feat for most people, who absolutely abhor conflict and will hold out to the very end, hoping in vain that the problem will somehow go away.

The culture and climate of your organization should vibrate with the idea that it's *not* okay to wait. Here are a few methods to help your employees report potential problems to you as well as helpful ways for you to collect it:

- Post suggestion boxes in discreet places.
- Create access to an anonymous, confidential (and protected) voice-mail reporting system.
- Create access to an anonymous, confidential (and protected) fax machine.
- Create access to an anonymous, confidential (and protected) E-Mail system.

The Myth of the Security Guard Blanket

In too many American companies and businesses, the term *security guard* is an oxymoron. If you are a ranking executive in an organization, responsible for millions and millions of dollars' worth of products, services, people, equipment, and assets, do you *really* feel safe and comfortable in the knowledge that when you go to bed at night, your firm is being guarded by the lowest bidder?

Gavin de Becker is quick to point out that the typical contract security guard is usually an underpaid worker with little or no training in security procedures. When company leaders choose to rely on this person to protect large portions of their assets, they're fooling themselves. The presence of security guards alone is not a cure-all for the kind of corporate security problems that appear today. As de Becker puts it:

> I have worked with large companies who have security guards and security operations which are a virtual waste of money. I have said, somewhat facetiously, "Why not take the $2 million you're spending on security personnel who aren't doing anything and put it into insurance?" I suggest to them that almost anything they do can't be any worse than what they're doing now.

He is not a believer in the "appearance" of good security as a way to send a message of safety to the people inside or outside the organization:

> Bad security gives the impression of peace of mind and gives the impression a secure feeling. Bad security or poorly managed security fools everyone except the perpetrators. I've asked individual security personnel, "What is your job?" or, "What are your responsibilities?" and the typical answer I get is, "To guard the place, to be here if something happens, to check ID badges, to take reports, and to do traffic control."

Indeed, if you look hard at what it is these security people really seem to be doing, it has very little to do with actual hands-on protection or enforcement of the company rules, not to mention city, state, or federal laws. Checking badges and opening locked gates is not "corporate security"; defending your company calls for a new mind-set that starts with whom you let come behind your walls in the first place.

To Gather the Most Honey, Don't Let the Bees Back Into the Hive

Just as real estate is about location, location, location, security at the corporate level is about access control, access control, access control. Gavin de Becker notes that most companies have the rules of access control reversed. It's not whom you let in that's important, it's whom you keep out.

> It's typical to hear the average security guard say, "Well, I know the people who ought to be let in here." And yet the number-one failure of security operations in companies is access control—that is, deciding who you want to be in your environment and then enforcing it. The guy who operates the electronic gate which lets the employees into the plant or who controls the electric door to let employees into the building very quickly comes to see his job as "It's my job to *admit* people." So when a man in a nice business suit comes to the door or the gate, his first thought tends to be, "Oh, here's a guy in a suit, he must be okay, because it's my job to *let people in.*" That is *not* his job. His job is to specifically *exclude* people. It is to admit the people who belong there and to exclude the 230 million other Americans who *don't* belong inside. Very quickly they come to say, "Someone's coming to the gate. It's my job to open the gate." No, your job is to keep the gate closed and to exclude people who don't belong there and to admit those who do. So, the job of the security guard is to find out who belongs here.

But before we lay complete blame on the poor security guard who may not have the training, work experience, salary, or even the life experience to know what is right or not, it's time to point the finger at the people who *are* responsible for nurturing this just-a-gatekeeper mentality: the company executives who employ these in-house or contract security guards. As de Becker explains:

> Poor access control is *not* the fault of the person at the gate buzzer; it's the fault of the people who have designed the program. For example, companies that refuse to use a companywide ID badge or credential, which is most U.S. firms, and yet expect the security guard at the front gate will be able to determine who belongs inside and who doesn't, are asking that guard to make extraordinarily sophisticated behavioral science assessments of individuals who come in the door.

Is this the way security operations are designed and managed at your facility? Consider the implications of the procedure, of allowing someone who may not even be on your payroll to make snap decisions and value judgments about who should be allowed to come into your plant, factory, or offices and walk freely. De Becker worries that this is the wrong approach to corporate self-defense:

> Ultimately these firms are taking their lowest-paid employee, their least-trained employee, who is very often no more than a scarecrow wearing a uniform, and saying, "We want *you* to make the decision about who comes in and who doesn't. In reality, the president or the CEO of the company ought to be part of that decision by helping to establish the policy about what level of people can come in and what criteria need to be applied to the people who come in.

Of course, this is not to say that the president or CEO needs to stand at the gate or the doorway with a clipboard in hand, saying, "You're okay, you can come in, you must stay out." Clearly, that is not the function of the symbolic and actual leader of the entire company. The leader should, however, become intimately involved in the safety and security measures that involve his or her firm.

> These days, it's not enough for you, as a top executive, manager, or human resource person, to say, "Access control is not in my job description. That's the role and function of the security people." Today, in fact, it *is* part of your job description. The safety and security of everyone in the organization should be a part of *everyone's* job description.

The employee who fails to stop or question a suspicious person inside his or her company is like the one who sees smoke billowing from behind a door and says, "I'll ignore that since I'm not a firefighter."

Deciding who should come into your facility should be simply a matter of who is:

- Expected (i.e., a bona fide appointment with someone from the organization)
- Predictable and appropriate (no clear-cut security risks, such as unsupervised children, teenagers, trespassers, emotionally disturbed transients, etc.)
- Belonging (people who have legitimate business with the company: real customers, vendors, and salespeople)

Access Control Versus Ego Control

The question of control over who gets inside, who must stay out, who may roam the building at will, and who must stay in one designated area is not without its difficulties, especially in terms of the indignation factor, which comes into play when employees, visitors, or vendors who have been forced to identify themselves feel offended and take it out on the security officer.

It's this kind of organizational peer pressure that ruins perfectly sound ideas. As Gavin de Becker puts it:

> If you fail to admit someone who should have been admitted, you will not get into trouble. If, however,

you admit someone who should not have been admitted, you'll be in the worst kind of trouble. It's too hard to get the toothpaste back into the tube.

Creating five seconds of inconvenience (asking people to display their badge ID cards and pin them to their coats) should be completely supported by the company and its leaders.

But what happens all too often in companies is that security people who are trained and given an access control post become what de Becker calls "brow-beaten victims." Within mere weeks of being given that job and the supposed guidance and direction needed to do it properly, they are chastised for failing to admit people who belong inside. Phrases like, "Don't you realize he's our biggest customer?" or "Don't you see that she's the head of our Dallas office?" ring out at the security desk. How would the security guard know this? Why should we expect this person to commit every "important" face to memory?

The Myth of the Access Control Policy and Procedure

In conversations and site-security reviews with his clients, Gavin de Becker frequently asks them for a written copy of their access control policy—i.e., who can come into the building, who cannot, who makes the decisions, at which levels, and why.

Fortunately, de Becker does not hold his breath while waiting for these pages, or he would turn 14 shades of blue. The point is that most companies do not have a written policy about access control. To complain about security problems in your firm without such a policy is to blame the unchained goat for eating your vegetable garden.

For Gavin de Becker, there is no such thing as an unwritten or informal security policy. Company executives who say, "We have a strict, zero-tolerance policy about data protection, workplace violence, employee theft, computer access, or entry into specific areas, etc.," and then actually have no *written* policy about these things are fooling themselves.

From a liability perspective and certainly from a courtroom view, to say that an unwritten, values-based, or normative policy exists is akin to not having one at all. Witness the following hypothetical but clearly possible courtroom exchange:

Plaintiff's attorney: *So, you're telling me that you allow just anyone into your company?*

Security director: *Well, no. Of course not!*

Plaintiff's attorney: *Then how was it that my client was injured by a disgruntled former employee who simply walked through the front door unchallenged?*

Security director: *We usually stop everyone that comes into the plant and check their ID. This person just slipped past us.*

Plaintiff's attorney: *Could you please show the court your written policy for access control? That is, the written procedures you use to decide who may come into the building and who may not.*

Security director: *Well, we really don't have a formal written policy. But everyone is fully aware of our security procedures . . .*

Plaintiff's attorney: *Including, I see, the person who got into the building without permission.*

Gavin de Becker sees this failing as one of the major liability issues surrounding the proper protection of people and assets:

> There is no such thing as a security policy that is not written down, except for what I call an "evolutionary policy," which appears and evolves and just becomes the policy. Based on certain observations I make, I can tell a company, "I know that it is the policy of your company to admit people who wear nice suits." That's the policy of the company because that's what's happening. What happens every day is, in fact, the policy. When something is allowed to happen, it is thus ratified. And then, indeed, it is the policy of the company.

So if the firm that has the unwritten or unspoken security policy of allowing any well-dressed white man, or any delivery drivers wearing uniforms with their names sewn over their pockets, or any important-looking people carrying clipboards or cellular phones or keyrings, that is what they will do. The key phrase that is left unsaid in this last statement is ". . . until something happens."

Until something goes wrong and the well-dressed white male turns out to be an industrial spy working for your competitor, a vandal, a homicidal workplace killer, a professional thief or robber, or a newly divorced man who wishes to shoot his former wife in front of her boss, nothing will change.

True corporate self-defense looks at a company as a living and breathing facility with people and assets that demand protection, sometimes from other people or events outside the firm's walls, and sometimes from people or events on the inside.

11

Think, Communicate, Change, and Learn

By perseverance the snail reached the ark.
—Charles Haddon Spurgeon

At this point, the feelings of some readers may range from grave apprehension to downright worry; others may experience a calm that comes from further understanding what they already knew from experience or suspected all along or a newfound sense of confidence based on a healthy injection of reality.

The discomfort felt by some readers may come from their discovery of some real truths about their companies and the respective liability factors, risk areas, and serious concerns. This new awareness of the potential problems their companies face from inside or outside may also stem from the sudden realization that their organizations, departments, executives, managers, and employees are for the most part unprepared for a potentially damaging event. It can be more than a bit difficult to make this kind of admission, either to others or yourself.

If you hold a position of power inside your organization—that is, you're responsible for important areas relating to the control of dollars, people, and assets—then no doubt your pride is tied up in your work. To admit that there are some flaws, weaknesses, or other glaring or not-so-evident areas of liability in your firm is somehow to admit fault, demonstrate that you're not as capable as you first thought or that you would not really know how to respond to a situation.

But perhaps it's better to see your current or potential problems now, when they may be more recognizable, manageable, and less damaging, than to wait for them to spring up in the middle of that fabled Sunday evening when no one is around the office save the janitors.

When NASA shoots a rocket toward Mars, they don't aim it where the planet is *now,* but rather, where it *will be* when the craft arrives. Event-specific planning and the thinking that goes with it calls for you to make the same kinds of predictions. "If X were to happen to our firm tomorrow, would we be in a position to handle it?"

As these cases and all the experts attest, corporate self-defense and problem management begins long before anything bad happens. The best plans for corporate safety, security, and sanity begin at the beginning. If you're prepared for the worst and it never arises, so much the better. But if you have no written plans, no people ready to initiate them, and no real sense of command and control over whatever part of the organization is in your care, you'll suffer. You *can* minimize the damage in even the worst corporate disasters, if you've planned ahead and committed the people and resources to those plans.

Communication Breakdowns: Management's Deaf Ears

By now, you should know that problems in business rarely fix themselves.

> One of the main values of prior crisis planning is that it serves to keep you in a proactive mind-set. Good crisis plans are not static; if you have to blow the dust off yours every five years, they're seriously out of date.

Your awareness of problems that arise either inside or outside your organization is linked to one key variable: communication. If you have your fingers on the internal and external pulses—that is, near your employees and your customers, vendors, outside business partners, competitors, and any other group who orbits your firm in the periphery, then you will be close to the source of any future situation.

Easy to say, hard to do? Yes, but only if you fail to understand the dynamics of business communication, which is:

> In order to know what is really going on in or around your organization, you must ask people direct questions.

This is not sarcasm, or a statement of the completely obvious, it's a reality. Most people do not volunteer information about potentially difficult events, even if the outcome may affect them directly.

Why? There may be many reasons. They may fear that they will be blamed, linked, or harmed by their release of this knowledge. They may have their own rationalizations for wanting to see you or your company fail (as with the disgruntled employee or whole department that sabotages customer relationships to "punish" the company). They may fear a kill-the-messenger response from you. And lastly, like most people they probably abhor conflict, dislike confrontation, and will go out of their way to avoid anything that jars them from their comfort zone.

This syndrome (better known as "if no one asks, I won't tell") exists in organizations where for many reasons, the culture does not encourage forthright talk, either between managers or between managers and their employees.

What about the honest employees, who see outright stealing going on at levels reaching thousands of dollars? Why don't they speak up about it, especially since these losses may affect the safety of their jobs or bonuses?

What about the employees, who see incidents of sexual harassment, racial strife, vandalism, sabotage, and threats or acts of workplace violence? Why don't they come forward, especially if the fears, lawsuits, or injuries that follow these events affect the safety of their jobs and paychecks?

What about the employees who see that certain products are defective—or worse, dangerous—and say nothing? What about the employees who see dangerous conditions, hazardous procedures, spills, or the possibility of serious accidents? Why don't they tell someone in a position of authority?

What of the vendors, longtime customers, and related business partners who may hear of trouble on the horizon, in the form of some kind of product, image, lawsuit, or outside agitator problem? Why don't they pick up the phone?

And finally, what about employees who are sharp enough to sense the general malaise, rampant unhappiness, or toxic culture flourishing inside the organization? Why do they not organize themselves and ask the people in power to stem the despondency?

In truth, the reasons behind all of these are two: (1) either no one ever asked them: or worse (2) the lines of communication and the method in which people communicate along traditional lines in the organization are flawed. We see "fiefdom management" at work. The various executives, department heads, managers, and first-line supervisors have built their own castles, complete with moats, dragons, and plenty of boiling oil to keep people at bay.

There are managers who say to employees, "Don't bother me with it unless it's a true 'work' problem," (read that as being strictly related to productions, outputs, quality, results, teams, customers, etc.). Such managers send a very clear message to everyone who wants to approach them with a concern that may not meet the excessively strict definition of "work" problem: Don't.

The supervisor who says, "Come to me with whatever problems are affecting your work performance and I'll promise to keep them confidential," and then who turns right around and leaks information, gossips, or otherwise acts unethically, tells employees that their personal lives are now everyone else's business.

The security manager who takes a number of theft or vandalism reports and then discreetly files them in the "Things to Be Dealt with Later" cabinet has told all future victims and suspects that the organization can't or won't help to prosecute the guilty and can't or won't protect the innocent.

Consider the production or plant supervisor who allows dangerous conditions to exist and who either discounts valid information (i.e., "It's not your job to worry about that, it's mine. You've told me, so now get back to work") or accuses the reporting employee of being a whistle-blower (i.e., "What are you trying to do, blow this whole contract for everybody?"). Don't such responses tell the employees that those who complain are held to a different, negative standard than those who don't?

> The point of all these horror stories is that the best people to help you see and later fix impending crises either inside or outside your organization are the ones who do most of the work.

One of the tenets of leadership is empowerment: your ability to empower your people to work hard and well without you having to guide them or watch their every move. And with this empowerment should come the sense that they can come to you with any concern that affects their work productivity or their perception of the organization's ongoing performance.

Consider your use of the following statement:

What is it about our relationship or the way we communicate that could be improved so that you would feel that you could come and talk to me at any time?

This is something you should ask the people who work for you at least two different times: once as a group and again on a one-on-one basis. The onus is on *you* to improve the communication process, not on the people who work for you.

Rest assured they won't volunteer a soliloquy for you as to what to do, but if you're able to impress upon them—together or alone in your office—that you *want* to be receptive, that they *can* trust you, that you *will* be discrete and ethical, and that you *must* hear from them if they see, hear, or discover problems, you can break down the usual communication barriers between employees and their bosses.

Build upon the future with your employees. Later, after one significant problem ends, another one may be on the horizon, and you and your people will all have to go back to work, both individually and as a team. By managing their feelings and making clear the reasons and methods they can use to communicate more effectively with you, you can lay the groundwork for more productive fact-finding discussions in the future.

You should want your employees to know, rain or shine, if they see, hear, or have a problem with another employee, a customer, a product, a policy or procedure, or any other issue relating to the good health of the company, they can come to you and talk about it. And even then, if you don't know, ask. If you don't learn what you need to know from one person, ask another, and so on, until you can put together a clear picture of what might be going on with the products or services you sell, or with problems relating to your employees, vendors, and customers.

This is not to say that you should grill your employees like Jack Webb in *Dragnet*, only that you should never perceive utter silence as a good thing. No news is *not* always good news. Just as it's best to check on small children and puppies when too much time has gone by between squeaks, if your employees or other outside sources aren't talking, there's usually a good reason for it.

> So-called unapproachable managers, who always seem to be "too busy" to talk with their employees, can do more of a disservice to their company than they will ever know.

A Little Healthy Paranoia Never Hurt Anyone

From a management problem-solving perspective, there are many pluses to taking a somewhat dubious look at business life. Were you to adopt a similar stance in your own observations of your organization and its potential for product, image, or employee-created crises, consider the advantages:

• You will always be in an "if-then" mode, so that even with a business problem of significant proportions, you'll never be without some kind of plan of action.

• Even if the steps you take are not perfect, they will be grounded in the sense of confidence that goes with the fact that they exist in the first place. (This comes from the school of thought that says, "I've already read the manual many times before, so I think can I fix things when they break.")

• Because other people in the organization (executives, managers, and employees) may look to you or you department for guidance in certain difficult situations, it always helps to look and feel the part for them. The director of corporate communications who can say, "I've already created boilerplate press releases for the following incidents" will inspire more confidence then the one who says, "I don't know. I've never handled that kind of thing before. What do you think?"

Of course, the negative side of being slightly paranoid about the health and safety of your company and its employees and assets goes like this:

• You may be perceived as the person who cries wolf too much (i.e., "Not another 'crisis discussion' from our glorified crisis management expert!")

• Top management may see you as a whistle-blower, a stirrer of the pot, or some form of rabble-rouser who brings up issues to the employers that are supposed to remain unspoken.

• You *can* go overboard in your perception of the world as a place that is out to do you and your company in.

While there are some problems to worry about and even more to plan for, it shouldn't distract you from your primary role in the company, which is serving your customers, helping your frontline people serve their external customers, or helping your people and department serve the company's internal customers.

Confronting the Comfort-Zone Manager

There is another risk to worrying about issues related to corporate self-defense. The main one is that most of your management co-workers don't want to hear about it. Their comfort zone, that place inside their heads where they hang their hats every working day—can get jostled and jiggled by too much doom-and-gloom talk around the organization. If they see you or your department as the primary source of tension, they may tune you out, or worse, sabotage your ideas or plans with top management.

The comfort-zone manager is the one who is afraid to go beyond or around the company's status quo. Such people, who have reached their position by holding onto the comfort of their routines, fall back on the old saw that too much change is bad. They may ignore valuable information derived from an organizational audit, dismiss risk analysis reports as overly dramatic, or otherwise choose to sidestep any data that might call for sweeping changes, especially in their own backyards. These people make a choice, whether it's conscious or not, to avoid any hint of pain. Their tactics include buck passing, blaming others, transferring people or assets away, or sidestepping difficult issues in the hopes they will disappear, go in another direction, or become someone else's concern. And in the worst case, their overwhelming desire to avoid minor pain for themselves (even if it means major pain for the organization) can trap other people into following suit. Sometimes, the person with the strongest personality, the best vocal cords, the most clout, or the most pervasive hidden agenda will sway others who may have originally agreed with the description or solution for the problem.

So what do you do with these people, especially if you're not in total control of the organization? How do you sidestep their sidesteps? Here, your cause should be one of the pioneer.

If you can't get other people onboard the crisis planning bandwagon, then leave without them. If you are the only one at your management level who sees the wisdom of planning for the future, then *be* the only one, live with it, and warm to your tasks. Sometimes tackling crisis planning situations reveals character in people. If you are the only one willing to put your forecasts, predictions, or plans to the test, then so be it. In good organizations, your work will not go unnoticed.

If you can't get support from your peers, go forward with your ideas and develop the necessary plans to protect or rescue as much of whatever it is you do control—a department, a work group, a division, etc.

If you're the only one who believes your firm needs contingency plans, draw them up and start a discussion about their use. If you can provide input into the necessary changes for your firm's policies and procedures manual, give it a try. If you have the ear of the security director, bend it. Don't wait for the dam to burst and then join in the finger-pointing or tedious displays of indecisiveness with everyone else who failed to anticipate, plan, train and practice, review, act, and react to any significant event.

And what if you are in a position to choose (and order) the people under you to start a crisis management response team, begin drawing up various contingency plans for problem events, or otherwise assess and react to the firm's potential liabilities? Your order of the day should be brief and to the point:

> *You're either with me on this or you're against me on this. I will only work with those who share my perception that we must create a proactive environment in this organization. We can and will react to crisis problems with preconceived, predetermined plans of action. We will start a review process that looks at our areas of greatest liability today. Once we determine where we may be weak, we will begin a controlled process to rectify those situations.*

To paraphrase Mark Twain, anyone will support you when times are good; it's getting help from people when times are tough that's important.

[If you can't find enough department heads, managers, or supervisors who share your vision about how and why to respond to real situations that may affect the well-being of your organization, its assets, customers, and employees, get new ones.]

Do Everything Right and They Still Might Not Believe You

We've reached a point in the book where I might want to wrap things up on an upbeat, positive note. But in the interests of breaking a trend, consider the following ending message:

[You can do everything right in a crisis, solve nearly every problem that arises, make lots of people happy, protect your company and its human and physical assets, and *still not* win the battle for your public's hearts and minds.]

The road back to corporate harmony and internal and external wellness is paved with boulder-sized obstacles. The public recognizes poorly executed crisis behavior when it sees it. People know when the leadership breaks down and the people in and around the organization have run amuck, literally or psychologically.

Firms under pressure tend to turn inward, circle the wagons, set up perimeters, lock the gates, and zip their collective lips. This "Leave us alone so we can fix this" policy only leads to more problems, as noted by this interesting piece of news:

According to a 1993 survey of 1,000 people by the New York PR firm Porter Novelli, Americans don't trust corporations to give them the truth in times of crisis. Corporate spokespeople, the survey said, are deemed the *"least believable"* by the public who views their work.

- Some 75 percent of the respondents said companies refuse to take responsibility for crises.
- Only 19 percent believed that companies are totally truthful in a crisis situation.

- Nearly 60 percent felt that companies either withhold relevant information or offer outright lies when a crisis hits them.
- And 95 percent of the people said they are more offended by a company lying about a crisis that about the actual crisis itself.
- When a company spokesperson says, "No comment," to a tough question, 65 percent of the respondents take that to mean *"guilty as charged."* (emphasis mine)
- The respondents thought that journalists were more trustworthy than business executives, 23 percent to 9 percent.

Finally, the survey group concluded that "corporate crises *do* have a lasting impact on consumers and affect their intent to purchase a company's products."[1]

This news is none too good, but it should come as no real surprise, especially in light of the current feeling by many customers and consumers that some businesses don't care much about meeting their needs or exceeding their expectations.

Practice ABL Management: Always Be Learning

If there is one philosophy you can take from this book, it should be this: if you're not prepared for change, you will be swept up by change.

Life in business teaches that few things are static. Customers change, markets change, and your products and service in response will change. The way you hire new employees should change to stay current with existing labor laws. The way you treat your employees should change as they learn and develop their duties. As you look around your organization, the list of policies, procedures, and processes that demand your attention is nearly uncountable.

It should come as little shock to you that many executives and managers find too much change uncomfortable. It may have taken them years to create their products and services, establish their firm as a dominant force in their respective markets, and build alliances with customers, vendors, and outside business partners. To suggest to them that one significant corporate problem could ruin all or most of what they've worked so hard to develop is akin to suggesting that the sun won't come up tomorrow.

If we haven't seen or experienced something firsthand, it can be difficult to understand how it will affect us or even *if* it will affect us. Crisis problems, many company leaders like to believe, have a way of happening at other companies, not ours. So if that's the case, let the other guy worry about how to save his firm from harm. We've got other jobs to do.

And in truth, maybe they are partially right, because significant events do happen infrequently. But stop to consider that your daily newspaper or favorite business magazine usually has at least one important story about a firm suffering through a crisis that has drained its time, energy, money, and resources; and these are just the ones we know about because of the publicity.

What about the countless companies all across the United States that are dealing with hard issues related to their people, products, or reputation—and that we never hear about? Wouldn't a scan of the civil court records in most metropolitan cities reveal numerous corporate defendants waiting for their day in court? And were it possible to check the major business insurance carriers, wouldn't we see numerous liability claims involving serious accidents, natural or man-made disasters, data or computer losses, thefts, frauds, and other policy-invoking damages?

In his memorable December 1941 speech President Franklin Delano Roosevelt had it only half right: We *do* have more to fear than fear itself; we have the endless possibility of a fearful event to keep us awake as well.

Every businessperson knows that risk is a part of corporate life. We take calculated risks every day based on the decisions, predictions, and hopes we have gathered to help us choose the right path. So why is it that the same gutsy, hell-bent leaders of a firm can make million-dollar decisions when the cards are in their favor and, out of sheer fear, can't move when a potentially devastating million-dollar loss heads their way?

The answer lies in their mind-set. If you were to ask most top executives and other corporate leaders in their fields, many feel they are untouchable. "Our company leads the world in the manufacture of X, or the delivery of Y, or the sales of Z. We are in the perfect position right now to thrive without limits and grow to even higher heights." This perception, while admirable and certainly something the employees and shareholders want to hear, is not without its perils.

As Peter Drucker so aptly put it, "Whom the Gods wish to punish, they first grant 40 years of business success." The point is, you can't have it all without paying hard for it at least once. Sometimes we cannot beg, buy, or borrow our way out of a serious setback; sometimes we have to go through the whole experience in order to learn the lesson.

If you don't learn from your past mistakes about hiring the right employee, you will repeat your errors with yet another inappropriate employee who later becomes first a detriment, then a liability.

If you do not install the latest safeguards, checks, and inspections when it comes to the design, manufacture, and use of your products, you will run the risk of an incident of tampering, sabotage, or accidental contamination.

If you do not evaluate and improve the way you train, treat, and promote your employees, you will start to see inappropriate behaviors from the marginal, immature, or opportunistic worker. The era of the worker who came to your facility, clocked in, did his or her job as told, and then left for home, has been replaced by that growing fraction of employees who bring their emotional baggage through the doors with them every day. To hope that they will leave, move, retire, quit, or get transferred to someone else's department is to avoid your need to intervene in their working lives when problems first surface. Issues that never came to the workplace as little as 10 years ago now affect the employees and their productivity and performance almost daily now.

Finally, your learning and changing processes must consider the sanctity of your firm's reputation. One wrong move during a highly publicized event can ruin what it took your company's founders decades to build. But just as Exxon will be forever linked with their grounded tanker and the makers of Tylenol will never fully leave their encounter with a cyanide killer, it is possible to do the right thing, minimize an already maximized situation, and get on with your business life.

Your approach to change in business lies in accepting it as real and even necessary. The techniques of effective corporate self-defense call for you to be flexible enough to recognize that change, while not always good, does indicate movement in other newer, better directions and growth and development for your company, its products, and its people.

If you can learn from your mistakes, extract the good from the bad stratetgies regarding the serious problems that have stricken your firm or others like yours, you'll be better prepared to deal with that great unknown we call the future.

Note

1. "In a Crisis, What You Say Isn't Always What the Public Hears," *Public Relations Journal,* September 1993, p. 10.

Bibliography

Albrecht, W. Steve, *Fraud* (Burr Ridge, Ill.: Irwin Professional Publishing, 1995).

Bliss, Edwin C., and Isamu S. Aoki, *Are Your Employees Stealing You Blind?* (San Diego: Pfeiffer, 1994).

Chappell, Tom, *The Soul of a Business* (New York: Bantam, 1993).

Cohen, William, A., *The Art of the Leader* (Englewood Cliffs, N.J.: Prentice Hall, 1990).

Coleman, James William, *The Criminal Elite* (New York: St. Martin's Press, 1989).

Dershowitz, Alan M., *The Abuse Excuse* (New York: Little, Brown, 1994).

Fink, Steven, *Crisis Management* (New York: AMACOM, 1986).

Gershman, Michael, *Getting It Right the Second Time* (Reading, Mass.: Addison-Wesley, 1990).

Grote, Dick, *Discipline Without Punishment* (New York: AMACOM, 1995).

Hamper, Ben, *Rivethead* (New York: Warner Books, 1986).

Joel, Lewin G., *Every Employee's Guide to the Law* (New York: Pantheon, 1993).

Klepper, Michael M., and Robert Gunther, *I'd Rather Die Than Give a Speech!* (Burr Ridge, Ill.: Irwin Professional Publishing, 1994).

Koon, Stacey C., and Robert Deitz, *Presumed Guilty* (Washington, D.C.: Regnery Gateway, 1992).

Levin, Jack, and James A. Fox, *Mass Murder: America's Growing Menace* (New York: Plenum, 1985).

Mantell, Michael, and Steve Albrecht, *Ticking Bombs* (Burr Ridge, Ill.: Irwin Professional Publishing, 1994).

Meilach, Dona Z., *Looking Great on Video* (Homewood, Ill.: Business One Irwin, 1993).

Miner, J., *People Problems* (New York: Random House, 1985).
Ramacitti, David F., *Do-It-Yourself Publicity* (New York: AMACOM, 1990).
Rubinstein, Jonathan, *City Police* (New York: Ballantine, 1973).
Sprouse, Martin, *Sabotaging the American Workplace* (San Francisco: Pressure Drop Press, 1992).

Index